5001 Names for Cats

5001 Names for Cats

Stephen Baker

With illustrations by Jackie Geyer

GRAMERCY BOOKS
NEW YORK

This 2006 edition is published by Gramercy Books, an imprint of Random House Value Publishing, a division of Random House, Inc., New York, by arrangement with McGraw-Hill Book Company.

Gramercy is a registered trademark and the colophon is a trademark of Random House, Inc.

Random House
New York • Toronto • London • Sydney • Auckland
www.randomhouse.com

Printed and bound in the United States of America

Interior book design by Stephen Baker

Library of Congress Cataloging-in-Publication Data

Baker, Stephen, 1921-
  5001 names for cats / Stephen Baker.—Rev. ed.
    p. cm.
  ISBN 0-517-22739-8
    1. Cats—Names. I. Title: Five thousand one names for cats. II. Title.
  SF442.4.B34 2006
  929.9'7—dc22

                                             2005045647

10 9 8 7 6 5 4 3 2 1

A few words of gratitude should go to my cat, Shakespeare, a smooth blend of Persian, Balinese, Japanese, Bobtail, Egyptian Mau, Burmese, Siamese, Manx, and, quite possibly, dachshund. It is this cat who supervised the preparation of this book while sitting on the back of the chair looking over my shoulder.

Stephen Baker

Author

Thanks to my two beloved companions, Tonka and Burma, whose curious habits made me *want* to find out by way of research if there were other cats like them. There were.

Scott Baker

Researcher/Writer

I would like to dedicate my illustrations to Jaba, Dickens, Butchie, Dara, Little Dickens, Eenie, Teger, J.B., Tonka, Tabby, Putsy, Ribby, Scratch, and Petie, who taught me everything there is to know about cats, and then some.

Jackie Geyer

Artist/Illustrator

Acknowledgments

Cats might have inspired this book, but it was people who put it together. There is a limit to what cats can do, their opinion notwithstanding.

I would first like to express my profound admiration to illustrator Jackie Geyer, who added a whole new—and beautiful—dimension to this volume. Her drawings speak for themselves. They show understanding between the artist and the cats in the world, the kind that only love can bring. But there's more to Jackie Geyer than that. This Pittsburgh-born artist is able to keep her cool under the most imperious pressure and deliver when promised—and at no compromise in quality. It was a delight to work with her.

Secondly, I would like to pay respect to my son, Scott, who spent much of his time between his school and office hours digging up vital information for this book. He has pored over dictionaries, history books, lists of names, literary works, almanacs—and asked hundreds of cat owners for their considered opinions on thousands of names. In addition, he edited the manuscript, deleting the bad jokes, saving the good ones, and adding a few of his own. You're a budding genius, Scott, a chip off the old block.

And who can forget all the other fine talent that made this book come to fruition? There's Gigi Pappas, who still believes in the old-fashioned work ethic; Lisa Grotheer, editor and expeditor at the publisher's trade book division, who went through the manuscript as if it were her own; and Gladys Justin Carr, Editor-in-Chief and Chairman of the Editorial Board at McGraw-Hill.

Too numerous to mention are the many friends, acquaintances, and strangers who were there when needed. They know who they are. My thanks for your kind—and expert—help.

Stephen Baker
July 1983
New York City

Contents

5001
Names
for Cats

Foreword

This book is for anyone who owns or ever expects to own a cat. It aims to solve one of the many dilemmas that confront all cat owners: how to arrive at a name acceptable to both the owner and the cat, though not necessarily in that order.

The fact is that no self-respecting cat likes to be called "Come here" or "Kitty, kitty, eat your dinner, nice kitty." Like people, cats prefer to be addressed by a given name. Not that a given name will make them get up and actually approach the caller—that's too much to expect. But it shows them that you think they are SOMEBODY.

Deciding on a name is no easy task, and it is a commitment that should not be made lightly. The cat's image of itself, and most certainly of you, will be dictated by your choice. An ill-conceived name is bound to affect a cat's social standing, not only in the company of humans but, more importantly, among other cats.

Several factors may enter into selection of a name. Like people, cats come in many shapes, sizes, weights, and colors, not to mention temperaments. Certainly you would not want to confuse your spaghetti-shaped animal by calling it "Meatball." Your jet black cat shouldn't be "Whitey," or your favorite giant "Peanut." Nor would you want your Jewish cat to amble through life with the name "Ave Maria" or your Roman Catholic pet as "Kosher." Such misnomers are sure to invite a serious identity crisis in later years, enough to drive the animal up the wall (a feat, incidentally, which cats perform with apparent ease).

Before you make up your mind, you may want to try out your idea of a name on the cat. Call out the name loud and clear. See what kind of reaction you get. If you're lucky, the cat will open one eye; and if you're very lucky, it will open both eyes. But don't let that discourage you. A show of disdain has long been a favorite ploy of cats. It clearly sets them apart from their major competitors, dogs, whose obsequious manners cats consider not only unbecoming but a complete waste of energy and time. Try again. And again. And again. Remember, you must give your cat time to grow <u>accustomed</u> to its name. A lifetime should do it.

This list of do's and don'ts may help to overcome your cat's initial objections.

1. Never call out its name while it is asleep.
2. Make sure you have reason to use the name. A cat would consider mealtime a good reason.
3. Do not, repeat, DO NOT bring up its name in association with things unpleasant—clawmarks on the furniture, a half-eaten house plant, an unraveled roll of toilet paper. . . . Such topics of conversation will not only bore the cat but aggravate its already low opinion of people in general.
4. Be careful to use the right tone in calling your cat. Cats resent being spoken to in a loud voice.
5. Try entertaining your cat. Lie down on the floor and roll over. Do a tap dance. Imitate a songbird. Don't try imitating the sound of a cat, however. Your idea of "meow" may strike your cat as ridiculous.
6. Should you offend your cat, take time to apologize.

Say that you had confused it with one of your human friends and you're very sorry about having committed so grievous an error.

7. Never make fun of your cat. Cats do have a sense of humor, of course, but theirs is more developed than ours. They despise cheap shots. For example, they find nothing funny about the "nine lives" cats are supposed to have, particularly if the storyteller tries to prove his or her point with a live demonstration. Expressions like "looks like a cat who swallowed a canary" strike them as plain silly. It implies guilt. Actually, a cat who has just swallowed a canary—or any bird—looks quite contented. It may even smile.

8. Pick a name that is different. If one name won't do, try stringing together two or three. Cats are fully aware that surnames and middle names are status symbols: such stately appellations appear in the corner of pedigree certificates. They particularly appreciate being called by their full titles in the presence of their peers.

9. Examples of names cats find totally unacceptable are Fido, Rover, Fifi (dogs' names) and John Doe (any human being can be called that).

The Talker

The Talker is never at a loss for words. Apparently, it has a lot on its mind. This cat is blessed with a surprisingly rich vocabulary. In addition to the word "meow," it uses such clever expressions as "mew," "mewl," and "miaow." Stringing these words together, the Talker then forms remarkably involved sentences. Often it takes the better part of an afternoon to finish a single one of them.

For the most part, the Talker prefers to speak from some kind of raised platform, so it can view its audience from above. Lacking a soapbox, refrigerator, or television set, the top of your head will do. The Talker cannot bear to be interrupted. It resents criticism, particularly in the form of thrown shoes. Catcalls it will not tolerate at all.

Arulo   [An international language]

Babel

Balbo   [From the Latin "Balbus," the indistinct speaker]

Bunkum

Chatty

Chin-chin

Churchill

Demosthenes   [Athenian orator]

Echo

Esperanto   [An international language]

Filibuster

Gabby

Glottis   [Opening of the larynx]

Jay   [Bird known for its constant chatter]

Larynx

Latimer   [From the Middle English "interpreter"]

Lingvo   [Lingvo Kosmopolita, an international language]

MacKenzie   [Nickname for the canned laughter machine used on TV]

Magnalia   [Latin for "mighty words"]

Melvin   [From the Old English "speech friend"]

Mirko   [Loquacious host gnome in Huygen Uill's <u>Secret of the Gnomes</u>]

Monologue

Mrs. Malaprop   [Character in Sheridan's <u>The Rivals</u> noted for her misapplication of words]

Myna

Pépé le Peu   [Wisecracking French skunk in cartoon movie]

Skelly   [From the Gaelic "storyteller"]

Tate   [North American Indian name meaning "a constant talker"]

Tattler

Tauky Tauny   [Talking tiger in <u>Captain Marvel</u> comics]

Windy

Winston   [Churchill]

Yakety   [-Yak]

The Devil Itself

Rumor has it that the Devil regularly appears on earth in the shape of a cat. That seems to be more than just a rumor.

There is strong evidence that many a cat has been sent up here from down under when the management there found its presence too much to cope with. People receiving the Devil Itself find themselves in much the same predicament, so they often suggest that it go back to where it came from. But this cat knows better than that.

Apep   [Egyptian king of the serpents with a poisonous bite]

Ara   [Greek goddess of destruction]

Azazel   [Standard-bearer of Satan in Paradise Lost]

Banshee [In Irish folklore, a female spirit who brings tidings of death]

Bogie [Spirit, assistant to the Devil]

Brimstone [Sulfur, often associated with hell]

Calamity

Charon [Ferryman on the river Styx]

Dahak [Babylonian dragon-spirit of death]

Diable [French for "devil"]

Diablo [Spanish for "devil"]

Diavolo [Italian for "devil"]

Dracula

Druaga [Babylonian master devil]

Duppy [West Indian evil spirit able to harm living beings by breathing on them]

Fury [Avenging spirit]

Hecate

Hellion

Hex

Hiisi [Finnish god of evil]

Horus [Egyptian god, "the avenger"]

Incubus [Evil spirit that comes at night]

Jinni [Being able to assume animal and human forms in Hindu mythology]
Jinx

Kobold [In German folklore, a spirit that haunts houses]

Loki [Scandinavian god of fire]

Louhi [Ruler of the evil land of Pohjola in Finnish mythology]

Maran [French evil spirit able to give people terrible nightmares]

Mongo [Evil planet in Flash Gordon comic strip]

Mumiai [Indian ghost fond of throwing objects around]

Mundunugy [East African]

Pazuzu [Evil spirit in the movie The Exorcist]

Peccata [Latin for "sins"]

Peccato [Italian for "sin"]

Petro [Dispenser of magic powers in voodoo rituals]

Poltergeist [Troublesome ghost]

Pyewacket [Cat allegedly a witch's familiar]

Sabrina [Teenage witch in comic strip]

Satanas [Latin for "devil"]

Sodom [Biblical city destroyed for its wickedness]

Utukko [A malevolent spirit so named by the ancient Assyrians; two others were Alu and Ekimmu]

Virika [Indian vampire that roams about at night making strange noises]

Voodoo

Zarbie [Dancing dervish]

NAMES FOR SATAN

Anathema	Cloot, Clootie	Dickens
Astarotte	Demon	Fang
Belial	Dennis	Halifax
Beelzebub	Deuce	Hoboken

Hornet	Ned	Scratch
Hornie	Old Bendy	Serpent
Jigeroo	Old Harry	Splitfoot
Lucifer	Old Nick	Tarsarus
Mephisto	Pickle	Thorn
Mephistopheles	Roundfoot	Titivil
		Tutivillus

GODS OF THE NETHERWORLD

Cora

Desponia

Hades [Greek]

Negral [Babylonian]

Orcus [Roman]

Osiris [Egyptian]

Persephone [Greek]

Pluto [Greek and Roman]

Tuoni [Finnish]

NAMES FOR HELL

Abaddon

Abyss

Amenti [Egyptian]

Aralu [Babylonian]

Avernus [A crater supposed to be the entrance to Hades]

Blazes

Blue Blazes

Gehenna

Hades

Halifax

Hoboken

Inferno

Jahannan   [Hindu]

Limbo   [Region between Heaven and Hell]

Naraka   [Hindu]

Pandemonium

Sam Hill

Sheol   [Hebrew]

Tartarus   [Greek]

RIVERS OF HELL

Acheron   [River of woe]

Cocytus   [River of wailing]

Lethe   [River of forgetfulness]

Phlegethon   [River of fire]

Styx

FURIES IN GREEK AND ROMAN MYTHOLOGY

Alecto

Erinys

Maegera

Tisiphone

VILLAINS

Ambrosio [The holy man who sells his soul to the Devil in Matthew Gregory Lew's The Monk]

Bandolero [Spanish for "bandit"]

Captain Nemo [Captain bent on destruction in Jules Verne's Twenty Thousand Leagues Under the Sea]

Councell [Captain Nemo's faithful servant]

Darth Vader [Evil lord in Star Wars]

Dr. Octopus [Of the comic strip Spiderman]

Dr. Sivana [Of the comic strip Captain Marvel]

Dr. Strangelove

Evillene [Evil witch in the musical The Wiz]

Faust [Sold his soul to the Devil in return for a life of luxury and sensual indulgence; var.: Faustus, Faustine]

Iago [Villain in Shakespeare's Othello]

Jesse James

J.R. [Ewing, of TV's Dallas]

Kaos [Evil organization in the TV series Get Smart]

Medusa [The Gorgon in Greek mythology able to turn people into stone]

Morgoth [Also Melkor, enemy of Iluvatar, the Creator, in Tolkien's Return of the King]

Mosca [Servant who hopes to inherit Volpone's fortune]

Nostromo [Unscrupulous protagonist in Nostromo by Joseph Conrad]

Peredonov [Paranoid hero symbolizing evil life in "The Little Demon" by Feodor Solgub]

Quotil   [Fly-eating evil in the videogame Yar's Revenge]

Rasputin   [Evil advisor to Alexandra, Czarina of Russia]

Svengali   [Hypnotist in Trilby by George du Maurier]

Tobor   [Captain Video's enemy in the TV series]

Volpone   [Avaricious protagonist in Ben Johnson's Volpone]

SUPERVILLAINS OF THE COMIC STRIP BATMAN

The Cat Woman   Hugo Strange   The Penguin

Clay-Face   The Joker   The Riddler

EVIL CREATURES IN THE GAME
DUNGEONS AND DRAGONS

Asmodeus   [Devil]   Juiblex   [Demon]

Baalzebul   [Devil]   Kurtumak   [Kobold]

Bahamot   [Dragon]   Orcus   [Demon]

Demogorgon   [Demon]   Tiamat   [Dragon]

Dispater   [Devil]   Varpak   [Ogre]

Geryon   [Devil]   Yeenoghu   [Demon]

Hrugjek   [Bugbear]

The Shape

Cats come in a variety of lengths and widths. There are big cats, small cats, rotund cats, square cats, elongated cats, short cats, tapered cats, flat-nosed cats, long-nosed cats, shapely cats, and unshapely cats.

All cats are able to change their shape at will and at a moment's notice. Depending on the circumstance, they become as flat as a pancake to slide easily under the throw rug, swell into a giant balloon to claim territory under your bedcover, fold in half to squeeze conveniently into the top drawer of your dresser, and stretch to twice their original length as they stand tiptoe on your chair to reach the food on the dining table.

Acantha   [Greek for "sharp pointed"]

Adina   [Hebrew for "voluptuous"]

Agnellotti   [Italian meat-stuffed dumplings]

Balloon

Banca   [A Filipino dug-out canoe]

Barge

Blimp

Blimpie

Bobbin

Brick

Bulk

Bungo   [Boat]

Calabash   [Gourd]

Cameron   [Gaelic for "crooked nose"]

Caravel [Old sailing vessel]

Chalice

Chassis

Copita [Spanish chimney-shaped glass]

Costilla [Spanish for "rib"]

Cube

Cubo [Spanish for "cube"]

Duffel

Dumpling

Egg Roll

Elmo [From the Teutonic "divine helmet"]

Filigree [Fanciful, ornate design]

Glob

Globoid

Gobs

Gordon [From the Old English "triangular hill"; var.: Gordy]

Gourd

Humpty-Dumpty

Jarro [Spanish for "jug"]

Jelly Roll

Jeroboam [108-ounce wine bottle]

Klops [German for "meatball"]

Knob

Knödel [German dumpling]

Magnum   [55-ounce wine bottle]

Manzo   [Italian for "beef"]

Marmalade

Marshmallow

Methusela   [216.4-ounce wine bottle]

Mota   [Spanish for "mound"]

Nariz   [Spanish for "nose"]

Nudel   [German for "noodle"]

Oblong

Octagon

Octopus

Pizza

Platillo   [Spanish for "saucer"]

Pompom

Polygon

Proteus   [Greek god capable of assuming variety of shapes]

Pudding

Puffball

Quadric

Quinlan   [From the Gaelic "well-formed"; var.: Quinn]

Redondo   [Spanish for "round"]

Rehoboam   [163-ounce wine bottle]

Rhombus

Roly

Satchel

Schnozzola [A large nose]

Stretch

Tamale

Tapioca

Tinaja [Spanish for "large earthenware jar"]

Toby [Drinking vessel]

Torso

Tuba

Tweedledee, Tweedledum [Characters in Alice in Wonderland]

Twiggy

Viola

Violin

Zeppelin

VEGETABLES

Artichoke

Asparago [Italian for "asparagus"]

Asparagus

Aubergine [Eggplant]

Avocado

Blumenkohl [German for "cauliflower"]

Broccoli

Calabaza [Spanish for "pumpkin"]

18

Cassava

Cavolo   [Italian for "cabbage"]

Cebolla   [Spanish for "onion"]

Celery

Chard

Cohombro   [Spanish for "cucumber"]

Cucumber

Fennel

Kale

Manioc

Micky   [Slang for "potato"]

Murphy   [Slang for "potato"]

Nettle

Parsnip

Patata   [Italian or Spanish for "potato"]

Pea

Pepino   [Spanish for "cucumber]

Pumpkin

Tomato

Turnip

Yam

Zucca   [Italian for "pumpkin"]

Zucchini

MUSHROOMS

Chanterelle

Morel

Parasol

Puffball

Truffle

FRUITS

Apple

Banano   [Italian for "banana"]

Cherimoya   [Central and South America]

Citron

Cocomero   [Italian for "watermelon"]

Coconut

Custard   [Soft apple]

Durian   [Southeast Asia]

Kumquat

Lichee

Loquat   [China and Japan]

Mango

Manzana   [Spanish for "apple"]

McIntosh

Papaw

Papaya

Pomegranate

Pompelmo [Italian for "grapefruit"]

Rambo [Apple]

Ranbutan [Southeast Asia]

Rhubarb

Ringo [Japanese for "apple"]

Roxbury [Apple]

Sapodilla [Central America]

PASTA

Anelli [Rings]

Cannelloni [Large hollow tubes]

Capellini [Fine, rounded, usually in nests]

Colorini [Colored macaroni]

Conchiglie [Shells]

Farfalle [Butterflies]

Fettucine [Flat thin noodles]

Fuselli [Twisted spaghetti]

Lasagne [Wide flat noodles]

Linguine [Narrow flat spaghetti]

Macaroni [Large tubes]

Orzo [Looks like rice]

Ravioli [Square]

Rigatoni [Large hollow tubes, ridged]

Spaghetti [Long rods, varied thicknesses]

Tagliatelle [Ribbons]

Vermicelli [Thin spaghetti, Italian for "worms"]

SAUSAGES

Abruzzi [Italian]

Bratwurst [German]

Chorizo [Spanish]

Coppa [Italian]

Knoblauch [German]

Kolasz [Hungarian]

Linguica [Portuguese]

Mortadella [Italian]

Pepperoni [Italian]

Salami [Italian]

Schinkerwurst [German]

Weisswurst [German]

Wurst

BREADS

Bagel

Baguette [French]

Biscuit

Brioche [French]

Buns

Challah [Jewish]

Corn Pone

Croissant [French]

Crumpet [British]

Dosa [Indian]

Grissini [Italian breadsticks]

Idli [Indian]

Kulich [Russian]

Matzo [Jewish]

Panettone [Italian]

Pappadum [Indian]

Pita [Middle Eastern]

Pretzel

Scone [British]

PANCAKES

Blini [Russian]

Blintze [Jewish]

Churck [Armenian]

Johnnycake [Southern United States]

Piroshki [Polish]

Suzette [Crêpe-suzette, French]

Taco [Mexican]

Tortilla [Mexican]

HAIRSTYLES

Bangs	**Crew-cut**
Boogie	**Flattop**
Butch	**Fuzzcut**
Chignon	**Swirl**

SHOES

Bootikin	**Oxford**	**Stogy**
Brogan	**Scuff**	**Wedgie**
Loafer	**Sneaker**	

CLOAKS AND COATS

Bolero	**Duster**	**Raglan**
Capote	**Mantilla**	**Spencer**
Chesterfield	**Poncho**	**Talma**

The Born Athlete

Incredible though it may seem, some cats show signs of activity between naps. Usually this entails little more than a slow, measured march from one location to another. Exceptions to the rule are cats eager to show off their athletic prowess.

Such a cat finds pleasure in sliding down bannisters, swinging on chandeliers, heaving pillows clear across the room, scampering up the nearest wall, leaping over sofas, beds, tables, and you—all to prove that you're dealing with Olympic Games material.

Atletico   [Italian for "athletic"]

Champ

Decathlon   [Athletic contest comprising ten track-and-field events]

Jock

Olympia   [Scene of ancient Olympic Games]

Pentathlon   [Athletic contest comprising five track-and-field events]

Stunts

Tarmangani   ["Tarzan" in ape language]

Tarzan

Wallenda   [Famous circus aerial acrobatic family]

THE BALLPLAYER

Blooper   [Lobbed pitch in baseball]

Bomb   [Shot at a basket from a distance]

Cager   [A basketball player]

Chucker   [A basketball player who shoots at the basket whenever he can]

Clip   [Block the opponent illegally by hitting from behind in football]

Duster [High, inside pitch in baseball]

Fungo [Batting-practice procedure]

Hoop [A basketball basket]

Knuckleball [Type of pitch in baseball]

Leaper [Basketball player able to jump high]

Looper [Short, high pass in football]

Pelé [Famous soccer player]

Pivot [Fast turn]

Plunge [Football player's leap into defensive line for short yardage]

Punt [Type of kick in football]

Roller [A ground ball in baseball]

Scatback [A nimble back in football]

Scramble [Improvised technique used by a quarterback unable to find a receiver]

Snap [Passing of the football between the legs of the center to the quarterback]

Spike [Slamming of the ball to the ground in football]

Stretch [Windup used by a pitcher]

Topspin [A rotation of the ball in tennis]

THE CLIMBER

Columpio [Spanish for "seat hanging from ropes"]

Jumar [Clamp attached to rope in mountain climbing]

Karabiner [Clip used in mountain climbing]

26

THE GYMNAST

Cabriole [Leap on the beam]

Cartwheel

Diamidov [Headstand on
parallel bars]

Hop [Form of landing]

Jeté [Leap from one
foot to another]

Stutz [Swing on
parallel bars]

Tinsica [Type of cartwheel]

Trampoline

Tumbler

Valdez [Backward tinsica]

THE JUMPER

Jackknife

Mollberg [Reverse somersault dive]

Pike [Bent diving position]

Twist [Sideways rotation in diving]

THE SLIDER

Arabesque [Stretched-out position in figure skating]

Blade [Hockey stick]

Christie [Turn in skiing]

Daffy [Riding two boards in skateboarding]

Flopper [A goaltender who sprawls on the ice]

Greek [Awkward skateboarder]

Heelie [Tail rotation in skateboarding]

Ruade [Turn in skiing]

Sitzmark [Mark left in snow by skier's fall]

Slalom [Zigzag course in skiing]

THE WRESTLER

Akido [Movements are mostly circular]

Budo [The way of a karate expert]

Dan [Grade of seniority achieved in judo]

Dojo [Karate school]

Hyoshi [Timing in karate]

Judo

Judoka [Judo practitioner]

Jujitsu

Jutsu [Karate technique]

Karate

Kata [Series of movements used in judo]

Keiko [Karate practice]

Kung Fu

Kuzushi [The moment of breaking the opponent's balance in judo]

Kyu [Grade of seniority achieved in judo]

Mudansha [Judo rank just below black belt]

Nagewaza [Throwing technique in karate]

Randori [Judo practice]

Shihan [Master in judo]

Tori [Thrower in judo]

Tsukuri [Technique of breaking an opponent's balance in judo]

Ukemi [Falling technique in judo]

Waza [Technique in judo]

Yoi [Fixed posture in karate]

The Singing Cat

Dogs bark, horses neigh, cows moo, birds twitter, but cats <u>sing</u>. Theirs is a melodious voice that ranges from the deepest bass to the shrillest soprano. Lucky is the owner—at least in the cat's opinion—afforded the opportunity to listen to his or her cat's musical recital.

There is no doubt in the Singing Cat's mind that its voice is vastly superior to that of any other living creature, most particularly human beings'. This is why you so often find this cat wherever there is music: next to the radio, in front of the television, or underfoot when you step out of the shower.

Adagio [Slow tempo]

Agitato [Musical direction: fast and stirring, agitated]

Aïda [Opera]

Allegro [Fast tempo]

Alto

Amati [Violin]

Amoroso [Musical style]

Andante [Slow tempo]

Apollo [Greek god of music]

Aria

Arioso [In the style of an aria]

Arpeggio [The playing of the tones of a chord in rapid succession]

Balalaika

Baldwin

Ballata [Italian song]

Banjo

Barbra Streisand

Barcarole [Venetian gondolier's song]

Baritone

Basso

Bassoon

Bebop [Style of jazz]

Beethoven

Bellini [Opera composer]

Bells

Bing

Bolero [Spanish dance]

Bon Bon [Singer George Tunnell]

Boogie-Woogie [Jazz piano style]

Brahms

Bravura [Brilliant technique or style in performance]

Brindisi [Italian drinking song]

Buffo [Male singer of comic opera]

Cadenza [Musical flourish]

Callas

Calliope

Calypso

Campana [Italian for "bell"]

Candide [Musical]

Cantabile [Musical direction: smooth, lyrical]

Cantata [Musical form]

Canto [Italian for "singing"]

Carillon

Carmen [Opera]

Carnegie

Carol

Carousel   [Musical]

Caruso

Celesta   [Instrument]

Chant

Cher

Chime

Clarion   [Small trumpet]

Clavier   [Keyboard instrument]

Cleo   [Lyre-playing muse in Greek mythology]

Coloratura   [Ornamental trills and runs in vocal music]

Como   [Perry Como]

Concertina   [Small accordion]

Concerto

Contralto

Coro   [Italian for "choir"]

Cricket

Cymbal

Debussy   [Composer]

Dolce   [Musical direction: sweetly]

Domingo   [Placido Domingo]

Doremi   [Do-Re-Mi]

Drum

Dulciana   [Organ stop with a tone like a stringed instrument]

Dylan

Elton   [Elton John]

Elvis   [Costello or Presley]

Enrico   [Enrico Caruso]

Ezio   [Ezio Pinza, opera star]

Erato   [Greek muse of music and poetry]

Euphonium   [Tubalike instrument]

Fantasia   [Free-form composition]

Fidelio   [Opera]

Figaro   [From The Barber of Seville and The Marriage of Figaro]

Fortissimo   [Musical direction: very loudly]

Gamelan   [Southeast Asian percussion orchestra]

Gigi   [Musical]

Glee   [Unaccompanied part song]

Glissando   [Gliding fingers over the piano]

Glockenspiel   [Instrument]

Grillon   [French for "cricket"]

Handel

Harmonica

Harmony

Harper   [Old English for "harp player"]

Heavy Metal   [Rock-music term]

Helicon   [Type of tuba]

Hendrix

Hootenanny [Gathering of folk singers]

Hurdy-Gurdy

Jazzy

Johnny Cash

Koto [Japanese stringed instrument]

Largo [Slow tempo]

Liberace

Libretto [Text of an opera]

Lily [Lily Pons, opera star]

Lohengrin [Opera]

Ludwig [Von Beethoven]

Lyre

Maestoso [Musical direction: majestically]

Maestro

Mandolin

Manon [Opera]

Maraca

Marietta [Naughty Marietta, musical show]

Marimba [Large xylophone]

Mellophone [Brass instrument]

Melodia [Greek for "melody"]

Melody

Mozart

34

Nat King Cole

Oboe

Ocarina

O'Malley   [Singing alley cat in the movie The Aristocats]

Oratorio   [Musical form]

Orpharion   [Instrument]

Orpheus   [Legendary Greek musician]

Pal Joey   [Musical]

Passacaglia   [Musical form]

Pianola   [Mechanical piano]

Piccolo

Polyhymnia   [Song and oratory muse]

Puccini   [Opera composer]

Punk

Recitativo   [Musical recitation]

Rigoletto   [Opera]

Ringo   [Starr]

Ritardando   [Musical direction: gradually slowing]

Roberta   [Peters, opera star]

Rondo   [Musical form]

Rossini   [Opera composer]

Ruckus

Salome   [Opera]

Sambuca   [Instrument]

Sarangi [Instrument]

Sarinda [Instrument]

Scherzando [Musical direction: playful]

Scherzo [Musical form]

Segno [Notation]

Serenata [Italian for "evening serenade"]

Simon [From the Hebrew "one who hears"]

Sinatra

Sirena [Variation of the mythical "siren"]

Sitar

Sonata

Sonny Bono

Soprano

Steinway

Stradivarius

Strauss

Tam-Tam [Instrument]

Tempo

Tenor

Terpsichore [Muse of dancing and choral singing]

Theorbo [Instrument]

Tin Pan [Tin Pan Alley]

Tom-Tom

Tommy Tucker [Nursery rhyme character who sings for his supper]

Tosca [Opera]

Treble [High-pitched]

Tremolo [Vibrato]

Trillo [Italian for "trill"]

Trovatore [Il Trovatore, opera]

Trumpet

Tutti [Ensemble passage]

Tympani [Instrument]

Victrola

Viola

Violino [Italian for "violin"]

Yoko [Yoko Ono]

Wagner

Yodel

The Speedster

This is a cat that wastes no time in transit. Determined to continue its twenty-four-hour nap with a minimum of interruption, the Speedster moves in a blur from the living room couch to the bed upstairs. This cat follows the old maxim that the shortest distance between two points is a straight line. Should some obstacle (a piece of furniture, you) stand in its path, the Speedster will either attack it head on, slip under it, go around it, or simply bounce over it as if it didn't exist at all.

Ace

Adidas   [Running shoes]

Aqueduct   [Race track]

Arrow

Atalanta   [Huntress in Greek mythology who agreed to marry a suitor able to outrun her]

Avanti [Italian for "forward"]

Belmont [Race track]

Bikila [Abebe Bikila, Ethiopian runner who won the Olympic marathon twice]

Blitz

Blue Streak

Boinger [A rear shock absorber in a motorcycle]

Bongo [African antelope]

Boyero [Spanish for "cowboy"]

Breakneck

Cannonball

Chassis

Cheetah

Chino [Leader of motorcycle gang in The Wild One]

Citation [Race horse]

Clip

Clipper

Coroebus   [Runner who was first recorded Olympic champion, in 776 B.C.]

Corso   [Italian for "course"]

Crash

Dodger

Dragster

Fanya   [Russian for "free one"]

Flash

Flit

Flurry

Fuego   [Spanish for "fire"]

Go-Go

Gonzalez   [Speedy Gonzalez, Mexican mouse in cartoons]

Grand Prix

Hightail

Hippity

Homer   [Home run]

Hotfoot

Hot Rod

Hotshot

Hurry-Scurry

Indy 500

Jackolope   [A cross between a jackrabbit and an antelope, supposedly found in Douglas, Wyoming]

Jack Robinson

Jiffy

Jockey

Jolt

Koni   [Shock absorber in racing cars]

Levina   [From the Old English "flash"]

Lickety-Split

Lightning

Lanza   [Spanish for "spear"]

Lulu   [North American Indian name meaning "rabbit"]

Mach   [Sonic speed]

Monaco

Nike

P.D.Q.

Pimlico   [Race track]

Pitapat

Presto

Pronto

Ralph   [From the Old English "swift wolf"; var.: Rolph, Raoul]

Rampage

Rapido   [Italian for "rapid"]

Remus   [Latin for "speedy motion"]

Ricochet

Ripper

Roadrunner

Rocket

Rush

Rusher

Schnippchen   [German for "snap of fingers"]

Scooter

Scramble

Sherwin   [From the Middle English "swift runner"]

Skedaddle

Slicks   [Tires without treads]

Snappy

Spectar   [Fast-moving smuggler in videogame Targ]

Speedy

Sprint

Spurt

Swifty

Targ   [Slithering jet in videogame Targ]

Thunder

Thunderbolt

Torque   [Twisting force]

Turbo   [Fast-moving videogame]

Wheelie

Whip

Whisk

Whiz

Whizz-bang   [A small-caliber high-speed shell]

Zap

Zigzag

Zing

Zingo

Zingy

Zip

Zipparoo

Zippy

Zoomer

AUTOMOBILES

Alfa Romeo

Arrow

A.S.A.

Barracuda

Beldone   [Futuristic automobile in The Patsy]

Bentley

Bugatti

Cadillac

Camaro

Chevelle

Clipper

Comet

Contessa

Cortina

Corvette

Cougar

Cutlass

Dart

Devin

Duesenberg

Edsel

Electra

Felicia

Ferrari

Fiat

Flint

Frazer

Gordini

Griffith

Jaguar

Maserati

Mazda

Mercury

Meteor

MG

Montego

Morgan	Sambar	Tempest
Opel	Serena	Tempo
Peugeot	Simca	Torino
Pobieda	Sprite	Volvo
Rambler	Stutz Bearcat	Yue Loong
Sabra	Swifty	Zim
	Tatra	

ROTATORS

Bobbin	Gyroscope	Spooly
Cater	Jack	Vortex
Gyro	Pinion	

WINDS AND WIND GODS

Aeolus [Ruler of the winds]

Afer [Southwest wind]

Auster [South wind]

Boreas [North wind]

Brisa [Spanish for "breeze"]

Canaca [Daughter of Greek god of wind]

Candelia [Spanish America]

Chinook [Western U.S.]

Cyclone

Eurus [East wind]

Favonius [West wind]

Gale

Harmattan [Western Africa]

Hotori [American Indian wind god]

Marut [Hindu wind spirit]

Notus [South wind]

Samiel [Middle Eastern deserts]

Sirocco [Mediterranean]

Solano [Spanish Mediterranean]

Tornado

Typhoon [In the tropics]

Vayu [Hindu myth]

Volturnus [East wind]

Wabun [East wind]

Whiff

Zephyr

Zephyrus [West wind]

The Flying Machine

Faster than a speeding bullet, more powerful than a locomotive, able to leap tall buildings in a single bound. Look! Up in the sky! It's a bird! It's a plane! It's the Flying Machine!

Curiously enough, this cat needs no wings to fly. It has the ability to take off vertically like a helicopter. Once airborne, it can perform an amazing variety of aerial maneuvers, such as diving into a tailspin and pulling out of it, sideslipping, looping the loop, nosing down, nosing up—and still come in for a perfect landing on all fours.

Airborne

Alario [Latin for "eaglelike"]

Aldora [From the Greek "winged gift"]

Alula [Latin for "winged one"]

Anila [Hindu wind god]

Anu [Babylonian god of the sky]

Arney [From the Old German "the eagle"]

Ava [From Latin "birdlike"]

Avion [French for "airplane"]

Captain Sparks [Fighter pilot in the <u>Little Orphan Annie</u> radio series]

Chewbacca [200-year-old Wookie, co-pilot of the Millennium Falcon]

Daedalus [Father of Icarus]

Dickory [Flying pig in Mother Goose story]

Emery [Airline express delivery service]

Evel [Evel Knievel]

Flubber [Magic mix that eliminated gravity in two Disney movies]

Frisbee

Galvin [Celtic for "sparrow"]

Icarus [Youth who flew too close to the sun in Greek mythology]

Jordan [From the Hebrew "descender"]

Kabul [Afghanistan airport]

Kamikaze

Lani [Hawaiian for "sky"]

Lizzy [Douglas "Wrong Way" Corrigan's airplane]

Marian [Anagram for "airman"]

Oops

Orbit

Pegasus

Picado [Spanish for "aerial dive"]

Radar

Red Baron

Rosa [Anagram for "soar"]

Rotor

Salto [Italian and Spanish for "leap"]

Shu [Egyptian god of the sky]

Skydiver

Sky King

Skywalker

Streaky [Superman's super cat]

Tumbler

UFO

Venera [Unmanned probe sent to Venus]

Yo-Yo

AIRLINES

Condor	Piedmont
Delta	Qantas
Lufthansa	Sabena
	Skipper

AIRPLANE NAMES

Airboy

Avenger

Bell X-1 [First airplane to break the sound barrier]

Brigand

Buzzard

Caravelle

Cessna

Clipper

Concorde

Convair

Corsair

DC-10 [Douglas]

Dynasoar

Electra [Lockheed]

Fireball

Flivver

Hawkeye

Nighthawk

Orion

Parasol

Piper

Sabre

Sea Bee

Sea Hawk

Sea Sprite

707, 727, 747, 767 [Boeing]

Silver Dart [Captain Midnight's airplane]

Skeeter [Tom Swift, Jr.,'s helicopter]

Skimmer

Skyhawk

Skylancer

Skymaster

Skystreak

Snipe

Song Bird [Sky King's airplane]

Spitfire

Talon

Tristar [Lockheed]

Turbojet

Twister

Victor

Vulcan

Vultur

CLOUDS

Cirro   [Italian for "cirrus"]

Cirrus

Cumulus

Nimbus

Nuvola   [Italian for "cloud"]

Stratus

ROCKETS, MISSILES, AND SATELLITES

Aerojet

Apollo

Asroc

Corvus

Ding Dong

Eagle

Firebee

Holy Moses

Loon

Luna

Minuteman

Nike

Polaris

Redeye

SAM   [Surface-to-air missile]

Snark

Sputnik

Talos

Titan

Viking

Zuni

The Little One

Every cat is small, cuddly, and adorable at the beginning of its career. Things change only later on. Some cats keep getting larger and larger as they gorge their way into adulthood and become Big Cats. Others choose to remain small, cuddly, and adorable and become Little Cats. Somehow they manage to look like kittens for the rest of their lives. This has many practical advantages. Unlike its more fully developed cousin, the Little One fits wherever there's room to spare: under pillows, in the mailbox, in filing cabinets, inside the piano, in sneakers, hibachis, air conditioners, TV sets, briefcases, shopping bags, stew pots, and cookie jars.

Abatwa [Legendary little people in Africa]

Alida [Latin for "little winged one"]

Alison [Gaelic for "little truthful one"; var.: Allie, Lissy]

Bantam

Barry Builer [The four-year-old kidnapped in <u>Close Encounters of the Third Kind</u>]

Baya [Spanish for "berry"]

BB

Beany

Bibelot [Trinket]

Bilbo [The Hobbit]

Button

Carlin [From the Gaelic "little champion"; var.: Carling]

Cerise [French for "cherry"]

Chico [Spanish for "small"]

Chiduku [Zimbabwe for "little one"]

Chippy

Chiquito, Chiquita [Spanish for "little one"]

Cipher

Cubby

52

Dab

Dinky

Doodlebug

Elvin   [Anglo-Saxon for "elfin"]

Fayette   [diminutive for Fay, meaning "little" in Old French]

Fleurette   [French for "little flower"]

Garbanzo   [Chickpea]

Gimli   [Dwarf in Tolkien's The Lord of the Rings]

Gram

Gremlin

Half Pint

Hobbit

Howell   [Old Welsh for "little alert one"]

Imp

Inky

Ion

Iota

Itty

Jack Jelf   [Nursery character]

Jen   [The Gelfing boy in The Dark Crystal]

Jerry Hall   [Nursery character]

Jigger

Jiminy   [Cricket]

Kane   [From the Gaelic "little warlike one"]

Keegan   [From the Gaelic "little fiery one"]

Ladybug

Lilliput

Lowell   [From the Old French "little wolf"]

Lunetta   [Italian for "little moon"]

Micro

Micron

Minny

Minutia

Miss Mowcher   [Dwarf in Dickens's David Copperfield]

Morsel

Muffet   [Little Miss Muffet]

Mugsy   [Juvenile delinquent played by Red Buttons in the TV series
     Comedy Variety]

Oncia   [Italian for "ounce"]

Pablo   [Latin for "little"]

Papoose

Paulo   [Latin for "little"; var.: Paula]

Peewee

Pezzettino   [Italian for "bit"]

Picadillo   [Spanish for "minced meat"]

Piccolo   [Italian for "little"]

Pinocchio

Pixie

Polly   [Little Polly]

Popcorn

Punta   [Spanish for "point"]

Pygmy

Ryan   [From the Gaelic "little king"]

Sanfor   [Short for sanforized]

Scintilla

Smidgen

Smurf   [Little blue being from Smurfland]

Speck

Spot

Stitch

Suzu   [Japanese for "little bell"]

Teeny

Thimble

Thumbelina

Tim   [Tiny Tim]

Tiny Tim

Tom Thumb

Tomtit

Urchin

Weeny

Widdy

Wisp

Witsy

Wyatt   [From the Old French "little warrior"]

NUTS

Almendra [Spanish for "almond"]

Almond

Cashew

Chestnut

Hazel(nut)

Mani [Spanish for "peanut"]

Peanut

Pecan

Pistachio

Walnut

SEEDS

Barley

Cardamom

Cumin

Fennel

Poppy

Sesame

SMALL CHANGE

Centavo [Mexico, Portugal, Argentina, etc.]

Centesimo [Italy]

Centime [France]

Centimo [Spain, Venezuela, etc.]

Chon [South Korea]

Florin [United Kingdom]

Groschen [Austria]

Kopeck [Russia]

Lira [Italy]

Penny

Piaster [Egypt]

Pfennig [Germany]

Shekel [Ancient Hebrew]

Shilling [United Kingdom]

Sou [France]

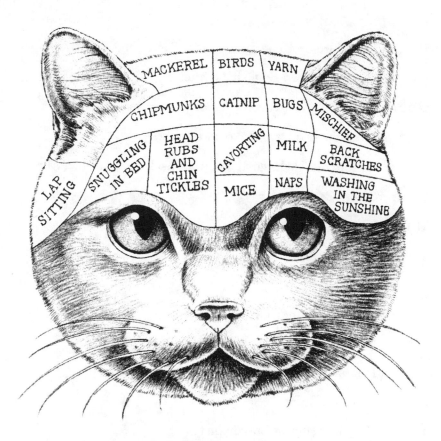

The image shows a cat's head with a phrenology-style diagram overlaid on the forehead, with the following labeled regions: MACKEREL, BIRDS, YARN, CHIPMUNKS, CATNIP, BUGS, MISCHIEF, SNUGGLING IN BED, HEAD RUBS AND CHIN TICKLES, CAVORTING, MILK, BACK SCRATCHES, LAP SITTING, MICE, NAPS, WASHING IN THE SUNSHINE

The Think Tank

Cats have a variety of important problems they must ponder. For example: how to get through a closed door, what's for supper, or how to keep another cat from moving into their turf.

The Think Tank likes to do its thinking in private. It does not welcome interruptions, however well intended. It is important that you respect its wishes: ideas are not easy to come by.

Closed eyes do not mean the Think Tank is asleep. They merely indicate that the cat is deep in thought.

Abacus

Ahimsa   [Hindu doctrine of harmlessness to all creatures popularized by Mahatma Gandhi]

57

Ajna [The "third eye" energy center in Tantra and Kundalini yoga]

Albert [From the Old English <u>Aethuelberht</u>, "the brilliant one"]

Albertus Magnus [Theologian and alchemist]

Aldo [From the Old German "old and wise"]

Alfred [From the Old English "good counselor"; var.: Alfie, Alfredo]

Alma Mater

Almanac

Alvis [From the Old Norse "all-wise"]

Amnesia

Archimedes [Mathematician]

Arhat [Tibetan for "a great sage"]

Arig [Turkish for "wise and intelligent"]

Asana [Yoga posture]

Asoka [Promulgator of Buddhism]

Athena [Greek goddess of wisdom and the arts; var.: Attie]

Au Courant [Informed on current affairs]

Brahman [Supreme source of the universe according to Hinduism]

Brian [Anagram for "brain"]

Buddha ["Enlightened one"]

Cabbalah [Jewish occult theosophy]

Cabeza [Spanish for "head"]

Canon

Catatonia [A symptom seen in schizophrenia]

Cerebrum

Chakra   [Energy center in Tantra and Kundalini yoga]

Channing   [From the Old English "knowing"]

Clark   [Latin for "scholarly, wise"; from the Old French clerc, "scholar"]

Clio   [Muse of history]

Cornelius   [Anagram for "reclusion"]

Daimoku   [A Buddhist chant]

Darwin

Deacon

Delphi   [Seat of the Grecian oracle]

Dictum

Disraeli

Dyana   [Sanskrit for "meditation"]

Edison

Edsel   [Anglo-Saxon for "profound thinker"]

Einstein

Elfreda   [From the Teutonic "very wise"]

Emerson

Encyclopedia

Engram   [Biological event thought to account for memory]

Erik   [Erik Erikson, psychoanalyst, first to use the term "identity crisis"]

Ernest, Ernestine   [From the Teutonic "earnest"]

Esprit   [Wit]

Eureka   [Greek for "I have found it!"]

Franklin

Freud

Galbraith

Galileo

Gandhi

Genio [Italian and Spanish for "genius"]

Guru

Gustav [Carl Gustav Jung]

Hiram [Hebrew for "most endowed one"]

Hobart [From the Old German "very brilliant"]

Hubert [From the Old German "brilliant mind"; var.: Hugh, Hube, Bert, Huberto, Huberta]

Hugh [From the Old English "intelligent"; var.: Huey, Hugo]

Hugo [Teutonic for "intelligent, wise"]

IQ [Intelligence Quotient]

Japa [Repetition of mantra in Japa Yoga]

Jefferson

Karma [Law of action and reaction in Buddhism and Hinduism]

Kopf [German for "head, intellect"]

Laputa [Land of scientists and philosophers satirized in Gulliver's Travels]

Leona [Anagram for "alone"]

Linus [Peanuts character]

Locke

Logic

Logica [Italian for "logic"]

Lotus [Basic Yoga position]

Luke [From the Latin Lucius, "messenger of knowledge"; var.: Lucas, Lukas]

Macrobius [Latin grammarian]

Magus [One of the Magi]

Mantra [Word of power in meditation]

Maxim

Maya [The power to produce illusions: Hinduism]

Memoria [Latin for "memory"]

Mendel [From the East Semitic "knowledge," "wise man"]

Mensa [Society composed of members with high IQs]

Mentor

Merlin [Magician and prophet who served as counselor to King Arthur]

Mesmer [Anton Mesmer, hypnotist who gave rise to the word "mesmerize"]

Milarepa [Eleventh-century Tibetan saint and meditator]

Mnemosyne [Goddess of memory, mother of the Muses]

Monica [From the Latin "advisor"; var.: Monique]

Motto

Mr. Chips

Nestor [Greek hero renowned for his wisdom]

Newton

Nirvana [State of complete bliss according to Hinduism]

Nobel [Alfred Nobel, chemist and inventor who endowed the Nobel Prizes]

Noggin

Norma [Latin for "precept"]

Oghma [Celtic god of knowledge]

Ollie [Owl in the comic strip Henry Hawk]

Om [Sound of the universe; when recited by a Yogi it produces inner harmony]

Orgone [Life energy]

Ouija [Talking board used to foretell the future]

Pavlov

Penseroso [Italian for "pensive"]

Professor

Prophet

Prudence [Latin for "prudent, foresighted"; var.: Prudy, Prudie]

Rorschach [Psychological test]

Samadhi [Sanskrit for "concentration"; state of superconsciousness in Raja yoga]

Sankara [Silence; suspension of will in Yoga]

Satori [State of enlightenment sought in Zen Buddhism]

Savant

Shanahan [From the Gaelic "sagacious one"]

Shannon [Gaelic for "little old wise man"]

Sigmund [Sigmund Freud]

Solomon

Sybil [From the Greek "prophetess"; var.: Sibby, Sybyl]

Thoreau

Thoth [Egyptian god of knowledge]

TM [Transcendental meditation]

Ultima [Latin for "distant, aloof one"]

Utopia

Waldo [Ralph Waldo Emerson]

Webster

Wilbur [From the Old German "brilliant one"]

Zarathustra [Prophet]

Zen [School of Buddhism]

PHILOSOPHERS

Anaxagoras	Hume	
Aquinas	Jaspers	
Aristippus	Kant	Plotinus
Aristotle	Leibnitz	Protagoras
Augustine	Lucretius	Pyrrho
Bonaventura	Machiavelli	Pythagoras
Cato	Marx	Santayana
Confucius	Melissus	Sartre
Descartes	Nietzsche	Schopenhauer
Diogenes	Parmenides	Seneca
Empedocles	Pascal	Socrates
Epicurus	Philo	Spinoza
Hobbes	Plato	Thales

The Big One

Big cats seem to get even bigger—and considerably heavier—when they fly through the air and land in your lap. And when they settle down for the night on your bed, they assume gigantic proportions.

The Big One can take up an entire chair, or even a couch, leaving no room for anything or anyone else, except possibly a small pillow or two.

Smaller animals treat the Big One with due respect. An exception is the mouse, who knows that size and swiftness do not necessarily go together.

Ampio   [Italian for "ample"]

Ana   [Elephant shown at the Republican National Convention in 1968]

Ancho   [Spanish for "broad"]

Arnold   [Schwarzenegger, body builder]

Atlas

Avalanche

Babar   [The Elephant]

Baloo   [Brown bear in Kipling's The Jungle Books]

Barnaby

Beaucoup   [French for "much"]

Ben   [800-pound grizzly bear, Ben Franklin]

Big Bird

Big Foot

Biggie

Big Mac

Bimbo   [Pet elephant in the TV series Circus Boy]

Bruto   [Spanish for "brute"]

Buster

Butch

Celeste   [Babar's wife]

Chi Chi   [London Zoo's giant panda]

Colossus

Cyclops

Dino   [Flintstones' dinosaur pet]

Dumbo   [Flying elephant]

Fafnir   [Dragon who guarded treasure of Nibelungs]

Gammera   [Giant prehistoric monster in Japanese film]

Gargantua

Goliath

Gordo   [Spanish for "fat"]

Grampus

Grant   [From the Middle English "great one"]

Grendel   [Monster slain by Beowulf]

Gross   [From the French "big, bulky"]

Grosso   [Italian for "big"]

Harvey   [Invisible six-foot rabbit]

Hector   [Eight-foot robot in movie Saturn 3]

Hefty

Hercules

Hunky

Hyperion   [A Titan]

Jottun   [Legendary Scandinavian giant]

Jumbo

King Kong

Loki   [Norse god]

Lothar   [Mandrake's giant partner]

Magna, Magnus

Magnum

Marcella   [Dancing elephant star of the Ringling Brothers' Circus]

Misha   [Russian mascot bear used in the 1980 Olympics]

Mishe-Mokwa   [Great bear in Longfellow's Song of Hiawatha]

Monstro   [Whale that trapped Pinocchio and Gepetto]

Mucchio   [Italian for "heap"]

Nessie   [Nickname for the Loch Ness monster]

Niagara   [Falls]

Orgoglio   [Giant overcome by Prince Arthur]

Oso   [Spanish for "bear"]

Pacco   [Italian for "package"]

Pallone   [Italian for "balloon"]

Polyphemus   [Cyclops in The Odyssey]

Samson

Sasha   [Bear in Hamm's beer commercial]

Shere Khan   [Boastful tiger in Kipling's The Jungle Books]

Skooku   [Elephant in movie cartoon series]

Snuffleupagus [Large elephantlike animal on TV's Sesame Street]

Sunja [First elephant to water-ski]

Surtur [Legendary Norse giant]

Titan, Titaness

Titus [Greek for "of the giants"]

Tony [Tiger used in Kellogg's advertising]

Toro [Spanish for "bull"]

Ursula [Latin for "she bear"]

Vasto [Italian for "wide"]

Waldo [Old German for "mighty"]

Whopper

The Literary Cat

This cat is a voracious reader. It reads newspapers, magazines, and books thoroughly and <u>aloud</u>, pronouncing most words as "meow." You must not, however, interpret this as a sign of a limited vocabulary. On the contrary, the fact that the cat is able to comprehend and actually translate English into Basic Feline attests to a superior intelligence.

Closeness to the printed word gives the Literary Cat a sense of intellectual participation. That is why you often find this cat sitting on a bookshelf posing as a bookend or perched on the carriage of the typewriter intently watching you when you're trying to write a book.

AUTHORS

Aesop	de Quincey, Thomas
Alger, Horatio	Dickens, Charles
Augustine	Dostoyevsky, Feodor
Baldwin, James	Doyle, Arthur Conan
Balzac, Honoré de	Eliot, T. S.
Boswell, James	Flaubert, Gustave
Browning, Robert	Fleming, Ian
Byron	Galsworthy, John
Camus, Albert	Glasgow, Ellen
Carnegie, Dale	Goethe
Cather, Willa	Gogol, Nikolai
Catullus [Roman poet]	Gorki, Maxim
Chaucer, Geoffrey	Hawthorne, Nathaniel
Cocteau, Jean	Herodotus
Cronin, A. J.	Holmes, Oliver Wendell

Horace

Huxley, Aldous

Johnson, Samuel

Kafka, Franz

Li-Po [Chinese poet]

Longfellow

Lucian [Greek satirist]

Machiavelli, Niccolò

Marcus Aurelius

Maupassant, Guy de

Nabokov, Vladimir

Naidur, Sarojini
 [Indian poet]

O'Hara, John

O. Henry

Orwell, George

Ovid

Petronius [Roman satirist]

Plutarch

Proust, Marcel

Raleigh, Walter

Rolland, Romain

Rossetti

Rousseau, Jean Jacques

Sakuntalla [Hindu poet]

Sandburg, Carl

Santayana, George

Sappho [Greek poetess]

Saroyan, William

Shakespeare

Sholokhov, Mikhail

Sitwell, Edith or Osbert

Spencer, Herbert

Spenser, Edmund

Spillane, Mickey

Tacitus

Tanizaki, Juni-chiro

Thackeray

Tolstoy, Leo

Virgil

Voltaire

Walpole, Horace

Whitman, Walt

Woollcott, Alexander

Xenophon

Zola, Emile

FICTIONAL CHARACTERS

Aladdin

Ali Baba

Amanda [Mother in The Glass Menagerie by Tennessee Williams]

Algonquin [Hotel in New York frequented by the literary set]

Amelia [Henry Fielding heroine]

Androcles [Protagonist of Androcles and the Lion by George Bernard Shaw]

Antigone [Sophocles heroine]

Armand [Lover in Camille by Alexandre Dumas]

Ben Gunn [Pirate in Treasure Island by Robert Louis Stevenson]

Camille [Alexandre Dumas heroine]

Candida [George Bernard Shaw heroine]

Candide [Voltaire hero]

Disko Troop [Skipper in Captains Courageous by Rudyard Kipling]

Emma [Jane Austen heroine]

Gulliver [Protagonist of Gulliver's Travels by Jonathan Swift]

Heathcliff [Protagonist of Wuthering Heights by Emily Brontë]

Hiawatha [Protagonist of The Song of Hiawatha by Henry Wadsworth Longfellow]

Huckleberry Finn [Mark Twain hero]

Juno [Irish housewife in Juno and the Paycock by Sean O'Casey]

Karamazov [Father in The Brothers Karamazov by Feodor Dostoyevsky]

Lavinia [Protagonist of Mourning Becomes Electra by Eugene O'Neill]

Leopold [Leopold Bloom in Ulysses by James Joyce]

Lonigan [Protagonist of Studs Lonigan by James T. Farrell]

Lord Jim [Joseph Conrad hero]

Mallison [Discontented captain in Lost Horizon by James Hilton]

Mendel [The hopeless "schlemiel" in one of Sholom Aleichem's stories of Chicago's South Side]

Nokomis [Daughter of the Moon in The Song of Hiawatha by Henry Wadsworth Longfellow]

Oblomov [Ivan Alexandrovich Goncharov protagonist]

Olyenin [Protagonist of The Cossacks by Leo Tolstoy]

Pamela [Samuel Richardson heroine]

Rebecca [Daphne du Maurier heroine]

Raskolnikov [Hero of Crime and Punishment by Feodor Dostoyevsky]

Rudkus [Jurgis Rudkus, protagonist of The Jungle by Upton Sinclair]

Sherlock [Sherlock Holmes, Arthur Conan Doyle protagonist]

Tchitchikov [Protagonist of Dead Souls by Nikolai Gogol]

Tess [Heroine of Tess of the D'Urbervilles by Thomas Hardy]

Trilby [George du Maurier protagonist]

SHAKESPEAREAN CHARACTERS

Celia [Duke Frederick's daughter in As You Like It]

Cymbeline [King of Britain in Cymbeline]

Dromio [Servant in The Comedy of Errors]

Falstaff [Jovial friend of Prince Hal in Henry IV]

Hamlet

Helena   [Heroine of All's Well That Ends Well]

Hippolyta   [Queen of the Amazons in A Midsummer Night's Dream]

Horatio   [Hamlet's friend]

Juliet

Katharina   [The shrew in The Taming of the Shrew]

Lafeu   [Old lord in All's Well That Ends Well]

Lepidus   [Triumvir in Antony and Cleopatra]

Macbeth

Oberon   [King of the fairies in A Midsummer Night's Dream]

Octavia   [Caesar's sister in Antony and Cleopatra]

Othello

Parolles   [Bragging knave in All's Well That Ends Well]

Pedro   [Claudio's patron in Much Ado About Nothing]

Petruchio   [Suitor in The Taming of the Shrew]

Polonius   [Meddlesome chancellor in Hamlet]

Portia   [Wealthy heiress in The Merchant of Venice]

Prospero   [Duke of Milan in The Tempest]

Puck   [Oberon's servant in A Midsummer Night's Dream]

Quince   [Carpenter in A Midsummer Night's Dream]

Romeo

Rosalind   [Heroine of As You Like It]

Snug   [Joiner in A Midsummer Night's Dream]

Titania   [Queen of the fairies in A Midsummer Night's Dream]

DICKENSIAN CHARACTERS

Ada   [Carstone's cousin and wife in Bleak House]

Bucket   [Detective in Bleak House]

Fagin   [Leader of den of thieves in Oliver Twist]

Gride   [Ralph's partner in Nicholas Nickleby]

Jaggers   [Lawyer in Great Expectations]

Jingle   [Villain in Pickwick Papers]

Jo   [Slum child in Bleak House]

Krook   [Rag dealer in Bleak House]

Madame Mantalini   [Dressmaker in Nicholas Nickleby]

Micawber   [The optimist in David Copperfield]

Miss Flite   [Crazed little woman in Bleak House]

Miss Knag   [Dressmaker's forewoman in Nicholas Nickleby]

Miss La Creevy   [Miniature painter in Nicholas Nickleby]

Nickleby   [Protagonist of Nicholas Nickleby]

Noggs   [Clerk and good friend in Nicholas Nickleby]

Pickwick   [Name of club in Pickwick Papers]

Pip   [Philip Pirrip, hero of Great Expectations]

Provis   [Alias of convict who becomes Pip's benefactor in Great Expectations]

Pumblechook   [Uncle in Great Expectations]

Sikes   [Thief in Oliver Twist]

Smike   [Crippled outcast at Squeers's school in Nicholas Nickleby]

Snodgrass   [Poet in Pickwick Papers]

Squeers   [Brutal schoolmaster in Nicholas Nickleby]

Twist [Oliver Twist]

Uriah [Uriah Heep, scoundrel in David Copperfield]

Wackford [Squeers's overfed son in Nicholas Nickleby]

Witterly [Hypochondriac woman in Nicholas Nickleby]

TYPEFACES

Aster	Florentine	Libra
Auriga	Futura	Melior
Basilia	Goudy	Metrolite
Bembo	Garamond	Optima
Bodoni	Harry Fat	Palatino
Bulmer	Harry Heavy	Pierrot
Caledonia	Harry Plain	Serifa
Caslon	Harry Thin	Stymie
Cheltenham	Helvetica	Trajanus
Clarendon	Icone	Trump
Corona	Janson	Vladimir
Egmont	Jenso	Waverly
Ehrhardt	Kaufmann	Wexford
Fairfield	Korinna	Windsor

The Monster

Monsters vary in appearance, but they all have one feature in common: a pair of glaring eyes. They may use these eyes to outstare you, or simply to glow eerily in the dark.

Scaring the life out of people is a favorite pastime of the Monster. It leaps upon people's shoulders with all the ferocity of a Bengal tiger. From there, it works its way to the top of the head for a better vantage point. Making full use of its claws, it then scampers down the back and legs of its victim. Never kick the Monster: it will kick you right back.

Abiku [Evil ghost in Africa]

Acheri [Troublesome ghost in the shape of a pale little girl as imagined by North American Indians]

Ankue [A shadowy gaunt figure believed to haunt the coasts of Brittany]

Annis [Black Annis, one-eyed hag of Scotland]

Arwe [Ethiopian serpent]

Azeman [Combination of vampire and werewolf supposedly growling in Surinam, a little country in South America]

Baba Yaga [Russian ogress]

Baka [Haitian ghoul]

Bantha [Giant monster in Star Wars]

Bay-kok [Red-eyed creature roaming among the Chippewa Indians]

Bergmonck [German word for "terrifying-looking"; gigantic monk]

Bigfoot [Huge, shaggy character that has been "observed" in the northern parts of North America]

Bodach [Shriveled old man of Scotland]

Bogey [Bogeyman; a goblin]

Boggart [Mischievous creature of England, no longer a threat to men because they're afraid of automobiles]

Bogle [A goblin]

Brute

Bugaboo [A source of fears]

Bunyip [Bellowing, ugly creature believed to inhabit rivers in Australia]

Burwor [Machéte-wielding denizen roaming the dungeons and labyrinths of Gilgamesh in the videogame Wizard of Wor]

Caliban [Progeny of the witch in The Tempest]

Charybdis [Water-spurting monster in Greek mythology]

Creeper [Horror character in three movies]

Cyclops [One-eyed giant in Greek mythology]

Dogai [Large-eared creature allegedly living on islands in the South Pacific]

Drude [Old English expression for a nightmare vision]

Fafnir [Wingless dragon in Scandinavian myth]

Fenrir [Wolflike monster in Scandinavian myth]

Firedrake [Winged dragon]

Flub-a-dub [Eight-animal combination creature of TV series Howdy Doody]

Fomorian [Misshapen giant that once terrorized the people of Ireland]

Frankenstein

Garthim [Giant monster in The Dark Crystal]

Gazook

Ghoul

Godzilla

Golem   [Statue turned into a huge terrifying figure creating havoc in Polish towns]

Gorgon   [Body-snatching alien creature in the videogame Gorgon]

Griffin   [A giant beast, part lion, part eagle]

Halpata   [Indian for "alligator"]

Harpy   [Ugly creature with a woman's head and a bird's body]

Hydra   [Nine-headed serpent in Greek myth]

Jumbie   [The zombie of the West Indies]

Kappa   [Wicked sprites from ancient Japan who were especially fond of cucumbers]

Kelpie   [Scottish man-eating ghost usually appearing as a mild-looking man or horse]

Khumbaba   [Horrible giant from Asia who was slain by the warrior Gilgamesh]

King Kong

Kraken   [Gigantic octopus "seen" by Norse sailors]

Lamia   [Mythological monster, part woman, part serpent]

Manticore   [Dangerous animal with the head of a man, tail of a snake, and body of a lion in ancient Greek legends]

Martian

Maul   [The giant in The Pilgrim's Progress]

Minotaur   [Half bull, half man]

Morg   [Man-eating monster in the videogame Tombstone City: 21st Century]

Mostro   [Italian for "monster"]

Ogopogo   [Giant creature supposedly living in parts of Canada]

Oni   [Ogre of old Japan]

Oonai [Melnibonean monster able to change shape]

Rakshasa [Hindu for "destroyer"—a potbellied, gorillalike creature]

Rusalka [Evil creature believed to be the ghost of a girl drowned]

Sasquatch [Another name for Bigfoot]

Scylla [Six-headed, sailor-eating sea monster]

Seeahtik [Another name for Bigfoot]

Siren [Enticing sea nymph in Greek mythology]

Skeksi [Evil creature in The Dark Crystal]

Sukuyan [A West Indian vampire]

Tapio [Temperamental fur-capped manlike creature said to live in the forests of Finland]

Taras [Sabre-toothed tiger tamed by the Tabar tribe in Burroughs's Tiger Girl]

Tarasque [A winged, scaly dragon feared by the people of Nerlue, France]

Tatso [Japanese for "monster"]

Umi Bozu [A Japanese sea phantom]

Vampire

Vetala [Vampire of ancient India]

Wampus

Wendigo [A Canadian horror, half phantom, half beast]

Werewolf

Worlock [Winged archenemy of the intruder in The Wizard of Oz]

Yeti [Abominable snowman in Tibet; an "all-destroying" thing]

Yuk [Mr. Yuk, the symbol of National Poison Center]

Zombie [Dead person given semblance of life by an evil force]

The Glutton

The Glutton considers eating to be by far the most important activity in life, if not the sole reason for it. Its notion of a regular eating schedule is simple enough: eating continuously all day. Despite the fact that it is a cat, the Glutton eats like a horse. It is even capable of making a pig of itself.

Anything swallowable is fine with this cat. Its favorites include sweat socks, cigarette butts, soap, plants, and any item served at the bottom of the kitchen garbage pail.

Abundalia   [Goddess of plenty]

Alma   [Latin for "nourishing"]

Apetito   [Spanish for "appetite"]

Appétit   [French for "appetite"]

Appetito   [Italian for "appetite"]

Arnold   [Pet pig in the TV series Green Acres]

Bistro

Bon Appétit

Boodle

Borscht   [Russian cabbage and beet soup]

Cacciucco   [Italian seafood stew]

Cantina   [Spanish for "eating place," "tavern"]

Carne   [Italian and Spanish for "meat"]

Casserole

Carnivore

Cavolo   [Italian for "cabbage"]

Chipster

Choppers

Chock

Chou   [French for "cabbage"]

Chuck

Cochino   [Spanish for "pig"]

Cola   [Also bureaucratese for "Cost Of Living Adjustment"]

Costato   [Italian for "rib steak"]

Costillas   [Spanish for "pork spareribs"]

Ensalada   [Spanish for "salad"]

Fabada   [Spanish for "stew"]

Fedilini   [Italian for "fine pasta"]

Fudge

Geschmort   [German for "stewed"]

Gorp

Goulash

Gumbo

Jambon   [French for "ham"]

Jaws

Kraut   [German for "cabbage"]

Lardo   [Spanish for "bacon"]

Lupus   [Wolf]

Lushwell   [Drunkard in cartoon]

Mulligan   [Stew]

Muncher

Munchie

Munchkin

Oakley   [Slang for a meal ticket]

Pac-cat

Piggie Wiggie   [Nursery rhyme]

Pizza

Porco   [Italian for "pork"]

Puchero   [Spanish meat and vegetable stew]

Python

Sauerkraut

Schnitzel   [German veal cutlet]

Seymour   [Man-eating plant in the TV series George of the Jungle]

Spud

Succotash

Tabaqui   [Jackal in Rudyard Kipling's The Jungle Books]

Tapioca

Toffee

Tum-tum

Tweedle-dee

Tweedle-dum

Wimpy   [Popeye's hungry friend]

Wocka   [Wocka-wocka-wocka, the munching sounds on Pac-man]

FAMOUS FAST-FOOD RESTAURANTS

Arby('s)   Julius   [Orange Julius]

Burger Chef   McDonald('s)

Burger King   Mr. Steak

Carvel   Ponderosa

Dairy Queen   Sambo

Dunkin   [Dunkin' Donuts]   Shakey('s)

Gino('s)   Wendy('s)

Hojo   [Howard Johnson's]

The Gourmet

The Gourmet is the counterpart of the Glutton. This cat picks
and chooses its meals only after thoroughly investigating them.
It will study the dish from every conceivable angle, and then
proceed to sniff at it for several minutes. Should the serving fail
to satisfy its culinary taste, the Gourmet will walk away from it
with obvious disgust and promptly go back to sleep to dream
about what the food should have been.

The Gourmet knows all about the importance of a properly prepared meal. It insists on a balanced diet and knows its best chance to get it is right from the family dining table. People, it knows only too well, rarely have plain cat food on the menu for supper.

Alacarte

Alamode

Antipasto

Baba   [French rum cake]

Baklava   [Greek pastry]

Biscotto   [Italian for "biscuit"]

Burrito

Canapé

Capocollo   [Seasoned pork shoulder or butt]

Caramel

Caviar

Chalupa   [Mexican dish]

Denis   [Anagram for "dines"]

Diablo   [Hot seasoning]

Dijon   [Type of mustard]

Eclair

Florentine   [French for a dish that includes spinach]

Fondue

Fudge

Ginger

Kampama   [Greek for "baby lamb"]

Kimchi   [Korean salad]

Macaroon

Marmalade

Masala   [Indian for "spicy"]

Melba

Mignon

Natilla   [Spanish cream]

O-cha   [Japanese green tea]

Oregano

Papaya

Parfait

Pastrami

Pâté

Pesto

Piccalilli   [Highly seasoned relish]

Pistachio

Prosciutto   [Italian ham]

Pul Koki   [Korean beef dish]

Romano

Sashimi   [Japanese sliced fish]

Sedna   [Eskimo goddess of food]

Strudel

Suimono   [Japanese clear soup]

Sushi [Japanese raw fish with rice]

Teriyaki

Tikka [Indian for "boneless chicken pieces"]

Truffle

Tutti-frutti

Yaki-nori [Japanese dried seaweed]

Yum-yum

Zucchini

CHEESES

Asiago [Italy]

Beaumont [France]

Brie [France]

Camembert [France]

Catello [Denmark]

Cheddar [Canada, England, U.S.]

Chiberta [France]

Corolle [France]

Danablu [Denmark]

Danbo [Denmark]

Fontina [Italy, Denmark, Sweden]

Gorgonzola [Italy]

Gouda [Holland]

Lefka [Norway]

Margotin [France]

Maribo [Denmark]

Mimolete [France]

Mozzarella [Italy]

Normana [Norway]

Parmesan [Italy, Argentina]

Pompador [Holland]

Provolone [Italy]

Rambol [France]

Ricotta [Italy, U.S.]

Roquefort

Saga [Denmark]

Samsoe [Denmark]

Sapsago [Switzerland]

Sardo [Argentina]

Segala [France]

Stilton [England]

WINES AND LIQUORS

Alava [Wine-producing area in Spain]

Ambrosia [Dubonnet aperitif]

Avignon [Wine-producing district in France]

Azura [Wine]

Barbaresco [Wine from Italy]

Barcelona [Wine-producing area in Spain]

Bardolino [Wine from Italy]

Barolo [Wine from Italy]

Barsac [Dessert wine]

Bordeaux [Wine-producing district in France]

Brunello [Wine from Italy]

Caballero [Cocktail]

Calvados

Carema [Wine from Italy]

Catalonia [Wine-producing area in Spain]

Chablis [Wine-producing district in France]

Chianti [Wine from Italy]

Cinzano [Italian wine]

Dubonnet

Fino [Type of sherry from Spain]

Glogg [Hot wine drink]

Madeira [Type of sherry from Spain]

Mendoza [Wine-producing plain in Argentina]

Montilla [Type of sherry from Spain]

Napa [Wine-producing valley in California]

Oloroso [Type of sherry from Spain]

Phoebe [Dubonnet aperitif]

Rickey [Brandy]

Sevilla [Brandy]

Sherry

Silverado [Sherry aperitif]

Soria   [Wine-producing area in Spain]

Spritzer

Täfelwein   [German for "table wine"]

Tarragona   [Wine-producing area in Spain]

Tintara   [Vineyard in Australia]

Toddy   [Hot brandy drink]

Torres   [Wine from Portugal]

Trocadero   [Vermouth aperitif]

Tuscany   [Wine-producing district in Italy]

Umbria   [Wine-producing district in Italy]

Veneto   [Wine-producing district in Italy]

FAMOUS RESTAURANTS

Amelio('s)   [San Francisco]

Ernie('s)   [San Francisco]

Fritzel's   [Chicago]

Koko('s)   [Phoenix]

La Scala   [Beverly Hills]

Le Bistro   [New York]

L'Escargot   [New York]

Lutèce   [New York]

Maxwell's Plum   [New York]

Orsini('s)   [New York]

Perino('s)   [Los Angeles]

Romanoff('s)   [Los Angeles]

Tony Sweets   [Miami]

HERBS

Angelica

Basil

Dill

Parsley

Rosemary

Sorrel

Tarragon

GRAPE VARIETIES (FOR WINES)

Barbera   [Italian origin]

Cabernet   [French origin]

Chardonnay   [French and Californian]

Gamay   [French and Californian]

Grenache   [French origin]

Merlot   [French origin]

Nebbiolo   [Italian origin]

Palomino   [Spanish and Californian]

Pinot Noir   [French and Californian]

Syrah   [French origin]

MIXED DRINKS

Benedictine	Margarita
Bloody Mary	Martini
Brandy	Negus
Collins	Pink Lady
Egg Nog	Rickey
Gimlet	Rob Roy
Highball	Rum Swizzle
Julep	Sherry Flip
Manhattan	Tequila

The Globetrotter

It is said that a cat is not an outgoing animal. Not so. Many cats like to go out—the farther away from home, the better.

The Globetrotter is a case in point. This cat has an uncanny ability to disappear at the exact moment you start looking for it. Naturally, there is always a good reason for its being out of shouting distance. The neighborhood refrigerators need checking out, garbage cans must be kept clean, and underground pipes must be looked into to see if they are wide enough to accommodate a cat's body. Mission accomplished, the Globetrotter usually heads home and eventually materializes on your doorstep flashing its best Cheshire Cat smile.

Andrew   [Anagram for "wander"]

Anvik   [Eskimo term for "going-out place"]

Avventura   [Italian for "adventure"]

AWOL

Axel   [Axel Heyst, wandering Swede in Joseph Conrad's Victory]

Bascomb   [Chauffeur in Harvey comics]

Bedouin

Bloom   [Leopold Bloom, wanderer in Ulysses]

Boris   [Russian for "stranger"]

Camino   [Spanish for "road"]

Convoy

Dora   [Anagram for "road"]

Easy Rider

Fanya   [From the Slavic "free"]

Ferdinand   [Gothic for "world-daring lover of travel"; var.: Fernando, Hernando]

Fernande   [From the Slavonic "adventurous in life"; fem. of Ferdinand]

Frances   [From the Teutonic "free"]

Franciscus   [Latin for "free man"]

Ganin   [Arabic for "vagabond"]

Gitano   [Spanish for "gypsy"]

Gypsy

Hobo

Hooky

Huck Finn

Jitneur, Jitneuse

Jitney

Jornada   [Spanish for "day's journey"]

Kon-Tiki   [Name of a famous raft]

Libero   [Italian for "free"]

Lone Ranger

Marathon

Maverick

Melissa   [Anagram for "aimless"]

Mosey

Nestor   [Greek for "departer" or "traveler"]

Nolan   [Protagonist in Edward Everett Hale's The Man Without a
   Country]

Odessa   [Greek for "odyssey"]

Odysseus

Odyssey

Orient Express

Paladin [Traveling gunman in the TV series]

Peregrine [Latin for "wanderer."; var.: Perry]

Pullman [Railroad car]

Quo Vadis [Latin for "where are you going?"]

Rodney [Anagram for "yonder"]

Roma [Latin for "wanderer"]

Rover

Santa Fe [Railroad]

Saracen [Nomad]

Scooter

Scrambola

Tao [Siamese cat in <u>The Incredible Journey</u>]

Telstar [Communications satellite]

Traipser

Trespass

Tripp [From the Old English "traveler"]

Vamoose

Wade [Anglo-Saxon for "wanderer"]

Wanda [From the Old German "the wanderer"; var.: Wendy, Wendeline]

Wanderjahr [German for "wanderer"]

Wendell [Teutonic for "wanderer"]

Zingaro [Italian for "gypsy"; var.: Zingara]

EXPLORERS

Captain Cook Captain of the Endeavour]

Columbus

Eric [Ericsson, the Red]

Livingstone, David

Magellan

Marco Polo

Raleigh, Sir Walter

Vespucci, Amerigo

The Darling

Everybody loves the Darling, especially the Darling itself. That's because the Darling is lovable, cuddlesome, caressable, kissable, and the pride of the family.

Not that this cat does not return affection in kind. Scratch its back and it will scratch yours. Chuck its chin and it will chuck yours. Tug its ears and it will tug yours. Run your fingers affectionately through its fur and it will run its claws affectionately through your hair.

Amado [Spanish for "beloved"]

Amanda [Latin for "worthy of love"]

Amorette [Latin for "sweetheart"]

Amy [Latin for "beloved"]

Anabel [Latin for "lovable one"]

Ananda [Hindu for "bliss"]

Andy Pandy

Angel

Angela [Old French for "angel"; var.: Angeline, Angelita]

Angelica [Italian for "angelic"; Latin for "angelic one"]

Anthony [Latin for "beyond praise"; var.: Antoine, Tony, Antonio, Antonius, Antonia]

Babe

Baby Blue

Bambina, Bambino [Italian for "baby"]

Barbie [Mattel doll]

Beatrice [Latin for "she brings joy"]

Bébé [French for "baby"]

Belle

Beryl [Hebrew for "jewel"]

Bibelot   [French for "trinket"]

Bijou   [French for "jewel"]

Billy Boy

Bo   [Chinese for "precious"]

Bon Bon

Bonnie   [Latin for "saved and good"]

Boopsie

Bouton   [French for "button"]

Brighteyes

Bunny

Bunnyfluff

Buster

Buttercup

Button

Candy

Cheri(e)   [French for "dear one"]

Chickadee

Chicky

Cho   [Japanese for "butterfly"]

Chuck

Cookie

Cottontail

Creampuff

Cuddles

Cupcake

Cutesie

Daisy [Anglo-Saxon for "the day's eye"]

David [Hebrew for "beloved"]

Dewey [From the Old Welsh "the beloved one"]

Dolci [Italian for "sweets"]

Dora [Greek derivation for "gift"]

Dulci [From the Latin "sweet"; var.: Dulcia, Dulcy]

Dumpling

Flopsy

Fluff

Fluffy

Gumdrop

Hedy [Greek for "pleasant," "sweet"]

Helado [Spanish for "ice cream"]

Honeybun

Honeypot

Honeysuckle

Isadora [Greek for "gift"]

Itsy-Poo

Jane [Hebrew for "God's gracious gift"]

Jellybean

Jesse [Hebrew for "God's gift"]

Jonas [Hebrew for "dove"]

Jonathan [Hebrew for "gift of God"]

Kevin [Gaelic for "gentle," "likable"]

Kiddo

Lily

Lollipop

Lucy [Latin for "light"]

Marshmallow

Mignon [French for "dainty," "darling,"; var.: Mignonette]

Muppet

Nathan [Hebrew for "gift"]

Nell

Nelly

Nene [Spanish for "baby," "dear little one"; var.: Nena]

Nougat

Paddington

Papillon [French for "butterfly"]

Parfait [From the French, an ice cream dessert]

Pastry

Peach

Peppermint

Pesca [Italian for "peach"]

Pixie

Polly

Posy

Princess

Pud [Scottish for "plump, healthy child"]

Pumpkin

Regalo [Spanish for "gift"]

Sabrina [Anglo-Saxon for "a princess"]

Sakura [Japanese for "cherry blossom"]

Sinclair [Latin for "saintly," "shining"]

Skippy

Smurf

Snooks ["Baby Snooks," comedienne Fanny Brice]

Snookums

Sterling [Teutonic for "good value"]

Sugarplum

Susie

Swee' Pea [Popeye's adopted son]

Sweetie

Sweetkins

Sweetums

Taffy [Old Welsh for "beloved one"; candy]

Theodora, Theodore [Greek for "God's divine gift"]

Theola [Greek for "heaven sent"]

Tompkin [Old English for "little Tom"]

Tommy

Toots

Très Bon

Tweedledee

Tweedledum

Tweets

Twinky

Ula [Celtic for "sea jewel"]

Vanessa [From the Greek "butterfly"; var.: Vannie, Vanny]

Winsome

The Warrior

Mindful of its territorial prerogatives, the Warrior will let any trespasser know where it stands. Its domain includes all the important places in the world: the neighbors' flowerbeds, the windowsill, sunny spots on the living room carpet, the top shelf in the cupboard, and the entire kitchen floor.

This is not to suggest that the Warrior is antisocial. It's only that, in the pursuit of justice, it has naturally accumulated its share of enemies: dogs and cats within a five-mile radius, and of course all squirrels, chipmunks, foxes, raccoons, skunks, rabbits, beavers, lizards, turtles, salamanders, birds, frogs, crickets, airplanes, cars, motorcycles, bicycles, postmen, policemen, the plumber, the electrician, the real estate broker, the insurance representative, the telephone repairman, family members, relatives, and any and all visitors who drop in to say hello. The Warrior does, however, have its circle of fast friends: the milkman and the garbage collector.

Abeja   [Spanish for "bee"]

Achilles   [Greek hero]

Aegis   [Shield]

Agamemnon   [Trojan warrior]

Alamo

Aleka   [Greek for "defender of mankind"]

Alexander   [Greek for "protector"; var.: Alex, Alexandra, Alexis, Sandy]

Alphonse   [Teutonic for "prepared for battle"]

Anhur   [Egyptian god of war]

Archibald   [Teutonic for "truly bold"]

Archie   [Antiaircraft gun]

Armada

Armageddon   [Battleground]

Armina   [From the Teutonic "warrior-maid"]

Arnold [From the Old German "mighty as an eagle"; var.: Arnaldo, Arnaud]

Aspero [Spanish for "rough"]

Attila [King of the Huns]

Bagheera [Panther in Rudyard Kipling's The Jungle Books]

Bahadar [Hindu for "brave"]

Bazooka

Ben Hur [A fictional early Christian]

Bernard [From the Old German "brave as a bear"; var.: Barney, Bernardo]

Bernice [From the Greek "she who brings victory"]

Biff

Big Bertha [German cannon]

Bismarck [German chancellor]

Bola [Missile weapon]

Bolo [Boxing punch so named by Kid Gavilan]

Boris [Slavic for "fighter"]

Bowie [Jim Bowie, soldier and frontiersman]

Bravura [Italian for "bravery"]

Brian [Celtic for "virtue," "honor," "bravery"]

Bunker Hill [Battleground]

Bushwhacker [Guerrilla]

Buster

Caleb [Hebrew leader]

Carney [From the Irish "brave soldier"]

110

Casey [From the Gaelic "brave"]

Castellan [Commander of a castle]

Cavalero [From the Spanish "dashing soldier," "knight"]

Cedric [From the Old English "battle chieftain"]

Chaperon [Protector of women]

Chauvin [Overly patriotic French soldier]

Chalmer [Teutonic for "king of the household"]

Chester [Latin for "of the fortified camp"]

Chevron [Insigne indicating rank]

Chutzpah [Yiddish for "gall"]

Clovis [Old German for "famous warrior"]

Collerico [Italian for "hot-tempered"]

Conrad [Teutonic for "brave counsel"]

Cornelius [Latin for "battlehorn"]

Constable

Cossack

Custer

Darcy [From the French "from the stronghold"]

Dinah [Slang for dynamite]

Dirk [Dagger or poignard]

Donald [Celtic for "ruler of the world"]

Donjon [Keep of a castle]

Donnybrook

Earl [Anglo-Saxon for "chief"]

Edmund [From the Old English "prosperous protector"; var.: Ned]

Edward [From the Old English "prosperous guardian"]

Egbert [Anglo-Saxon for "bright and shining sword"]

El Cid

Emir

Eric [Teutonic for "kingly"]

Excalibur [King Arthur's sword]

Farrell [Celtic for "the valorous one"]

Fearless

Ferguson [British rifle of the seventeenth century]

Fierro [Spanish for "iron"]

Foster [Teutonic for "keeper of the preserve"]

Garroway [From the Old English "spear warrior"]

Genghis Khan

Gerard [Old German for "spear mighty"]

Gideon [Hebrew for "brave warrior"]

Gilgamesh [Babylonian tyrant fond of wrestling]

Gregory [Greek for "vigilant"]

Gunther [Old Norse for "battle-army"]

Gurkha [Hindu soldier]

Hagen [Knight in Nibelungenlied invulnerable except for one spot
between his shoulder blades]

Harold [Anglo-Saxon for "army commander"]

Harvey [From the Old German "army warrior"]

Hawkeye [Hero of The Last of the Mohicans]

Hector [Trojan warrior]

Henry [Old German for "warrior"]

Herbert [From the Old German "glorious warrior"; var.: Herb, Herbie, Bert, Erberto]

Herman [From the Old German "noble warrior"; var.: Hermie, Hermann, Armand, Ermanno]

Herod [King of Judea]

Hessian [Mercenary used by British in American Revolution]

Hildebrand [From the Old German "war sword"]

Howard [Teutonic for "chief guardian"]

Howitzer [Cannon]

Hun

Igor [Scandinavian for "hero"]

Intrepid

Ivanhoe [Fictional Crusader]

Jarvis [From the Old German "keen with the spear"]

Jericho [Where biblical walls tumbled]

Jerry [German soldier]

Juggernaut [An overpowering destructive force or object]

Keith [From the Gaelic "from the battle place"]

Kelly [From the Gaelic "brave warrior"]

Kendrick [Anglo-Saxon for "royal ruler"]

Kimball [Anglo-Saxon for "royally brave"]

Kingsley [From the Old English "belonging to the king"]

Knight

Kozuka [Small Japanese knife]

Kubla Khan [Chinese emperor]

Lancer

Lawrence [Latin for "crowned with laurel"; var.: Larry, Lorry, Lorenzo]

Leo [Latin for "lion"; var.: Leon, Leonie]

Leona [Latin for "lioness"]

Leonard [From the Old Frankish "bold as a lion"; var.: Leonardo, Lenny, Linus]

Leopold [Teutonic for "brave for the people"]

Lester [Anglo-Saxon for "from the army or camp"]

Lionel [Old French for "young lion"]

Long Tom [Gun]

Lothar [An ancient warrior]

Louis [From the Old German "renowned warrior"; var.: Louisa, Louise, Lowell, Ludwig]

Luger [Gun]

Luther [From the Old German "famous warrior"]

Macbeth [Victorious Scottish warrior and misguided king in Shakespeare's play]

Madison [Teutonic for "mighty in battle"]

Malvin [Celtic for "chief"; var.: Melvin]

Marauder

Mark [Latin for "a warrior"; var.: Marc, Marco, Marcus, Marck, Martin, Marty]

Marshall

Martello   [Defense tower built along coastlines]

Maud   [From the Teutonic "mighty in battle"]

Maximilian   [Latin for "the greatest"; var.: Maxim, Max, Maxie]

McCoy

Mean Joe   [Nickname of a football player]

Merrimac   [Iron battleship]

Mincemeat

Napoleon

Nicholas   [Greek for "victorious army"; var.: Nicky, Nicolo, Nicolas]

Numair   [Arabic for "panther"]

Osborn   [From the Old English "divine warrior"]

Oscar   [Anglo-Saxon for "divine spear"]

Owen   [Celtic for "young warrior"]

Paladin   [Paragon of knighthood]

Panther

Panzer   [Armored tank]

Patton

Pedro   [Pedro Romero, handsome bullfighter in The Sun Also Rises]

Picador   [Bullfighter on horseback]

Poilu   [French front-line soldier]

Ponta   [Pugilist John Ponta in Jack London's The Game]

Puma

Ranger

Rebel

Remington   [American rifle]

Redmond   [Teutonic for "protector"]

Riley   [From the Gaelic "valiant"]

Robin Hood

Rocky

Rodenca   [Teutonic for "ruler" or "princess"]

Roderick   [From the Old German "famous ruler"; var.: Broderick, Ricky, Rodrigo]

Roger   [Teutonic for "famous warrior"]

Rudolph   [From the Old German "famous wolf," suggesting daring and courage; var.: Rodolfo, Rollo, Rudolf, Rudy]

Salvo

Savage

Saya   [Japanese scabbard]

Shing   [Chinese for "victory"]

Siegfried   [Medieval warrior with a magical cap; var.: Sigismondo, Sigismundo]

Sir Galahad   [Arthurian hero dressed in white armor]

Sitting Bull   [Indian chief]

Sloan   [From the Gaelic "warrior"]

Smasher

Socko

Spitball

Stanley [Slavonic for "pride of the camp"]

Tanto [Japanese short sword]

Thaddeus [Latin for "courageous"]

Theobold [From the Old English "boldest of the people"]

Thera [Greek for "untamed"]

Thora [Teutonic for "thunder"]

TNT

Toledo [Type of blade]

Tommy Atkins [British soldier]

Torero [Bullfighter on foot]

Toro [Spanish for "bull"]

Torpedo

Trigger

Trooper

Ulysses [Greek for "angry one"]

Valentine [Latin for "valorous"; var.: Valiant]

Victor [Latin for "the conqueror"]

Vincent [Latin for "conqueror"]

Walter [From the Teutonic "mighty warrior"; var.: Wally, Walt]

Warner [From the Old German "defending warrior"]

Warren [Teutonic for "game warden"]

Warrick [Teutonic for "strong ruler"]

Waterloo

Wilhelm   [King of Prussia]

Willard   [From the Old English "brave"]

William   [Teutonic for "determined protector"; var.: Wilhelm, Willis, Bill, Billy, Will, Willy]

Winchester   [American rifle]

Wrangler

Xenophon   [Greek general who fought Cyrus, circa 400 B.C.]

Zampa   [Italian for "paw"]

The Living Legend

More than any other type of cat, the Living Legend responds to its name, sometimes even pricking up its ears. This is in deference to the cat who inspired the name in the first place.

Every cat knows that there is no such thing as an "ordinary cat." The world in fact is filled with cats who have made their mark. Cats take pride in their brothers' and sisters' achievements and find particular comfort in the fact that many cats have become more famous than the people who own them.

Azriel   [Smurf-hating cat]

Beauregard   [Tiger in the comic strip Pogo]

Boo   [Pet cat in the TV cartoon The Funky Phantom]

Boo-Boo Kitty   [Stuffed toy cat in the TV series Laverne and Shirley]

Boots   [Bunny Olsen's pet cat in the TV series Gomer Pyle, U.S.M.C.]

Butch   [Pet cat in the movie The Incredible Shrinking Man]

Dinah   [Alice's cat in Alice in Wonderland]

Elsa   [Lioness raised by Joy and George Adamson, as chronicled in Born Free]

Ergo   [Mascot in the TV series Quake]

Geraldine   [Pet cat in the TV series Lum 'n' Abner]

Hecate   [Greek divinity who adapted a catlike mien]

Hope   [Cat's name in the comic strip The Gumps]

Italia Bella   [Mussolini's pet lion]

Jake   [Feline in the movie The Cat from Outer Space]

Jason   [Star of BBC's Blue Peter]

Jones   [Yellow tomcat in the movie Alien]

Kit Kat   [Pet lion in the TV series The Addams Family]

Max   [Pet cat in the comic strip Superman]

Morris   [Cat in commercial for "9-Lives"]

Muezza [Mohammed's favorite cat]

Orlando [Kathleen Hale's "Marmalade Cat"]

Puff [Dick and Jane's cat in primary readers]

Rhubar [Movie-star tabby]

Sabor [Tiger in Tarzan novels]

Saha [The protagonist in Colette's famous novel]

Salem [Cat in the comic strip Sabrina]

Solomon [Cat of Diamonds Are Forever and Clockwork Orange
    fame]

Streaky [Superman's super cat]

Tobermory [The talking cat in Saki's The Cat]

Tom Kitten [From Peter Rabbit story]

Tonto [From the movie Harry and Tonto]

Tigger [Tiger in Winnie the Pooh]

FROM OLD POSSUM'S BOOK OF PRACTICAL CATS

Alonzo	Grizabella	Pouncival
Asparagus	Growltiger	Rum Tum Tugger
Bombalurina	Jellylorum	Rumpleteazer
Bustopher Jones	Jennyanydots	Rumpus Cat
Carbucketty	Macavity	Sillabub
Cassandra	Mistoffelees	Skimbleshanks
Coricopat	Mungojerrie	Tantomile
Demeter	Munkustrap	Tumblebrutus
Etcetera	Old Deuteronomy	Victoria
Griddlebone	Plato	

A Cat Is a Cat Is a Cat

Contrary to popular opinion, cats don't mind at all if they are called "cat." In fact, they're proud to belong to the distinguished family <u>Felidae</u>. It's the owners who feel that the use of the word shows lack of imagination. If you happen to feel that way yourself, here are some combinations that will ease your mind—and still call your cat . . . well, cat.

Cataclysm	Catcall	Cattail
Catacomb	Catchall	Catty-Corner
Catalina	Catcher	Chessycat [Cheshire cat]
Catalonia	Caterpillar	Hepcat [Slang for dancer]
Catalpa	Caterwauler	Kittycorner
Catalyst	Catharine	Pussycat
Catamaran	Catharsis	Scat
Catamount	Catkin	Splintercat [Legendary
Catapult	Cato	flying cat of the woods]
Catastrophe	Catskill	Tigercat [Airplane name]
Catatonia	Catspaw	Tom [Short for "Tomcat"]
Catawba	Catsup	Wildcat [Airplane name]

THEY TOO HAVE A NAME FOR IT

Catálogo [Spanish]

Chat [French]

Felida(e) [Latin for "cat"]

Felix [Latin for "cat"; also "lucky one." Over seventy saints were named Felix]

Gato   [Spanish and Portuguese]

Gattaff   [Portuguese for "tomcat"]

Gatto   [Italian]

Katalog   [Yiddish]

Kato   [Esperanto]

Katze   [German]

Kedi   [Turkish]

Koshka   [Russian]

Mao   [Chinese]

Neko   [Japanese]

Olena   [Russian for "cat"]

Paka   [Swahili]

Color Me Beautiful

Cats come in many colors and shades—white, black, gray, yellow, red, brown, and colors God created specifically for them, probably when He had nothing better to do. Cats' coats also seem to encompass all conceivable patterns, except—as of this writing—checkerboards and polka dots.

Names of colors are very popular with cats; they give cats a sense of identity and, more importantly, hope that their owners will not confuse them with some other cat or, worse still, with a dog in the same household.

BLACKISH

Adria   [Latin for "dark one"]

Adrian   [Spanish for "dark one"; var.: Adriano]

Afro

After-Six

Blackbeard   [Pirate]

Blackie

Black tie

Brenna   [Celtic for "maiden with black or raven hair"]

Carbon

Carbone   [Italian for "coal"]

Charbon   [French for "coal"]

Dolan   [From Gaelic "black-haired"]

Donnelley   [From Gaelic "dark and brave"]

Dooley   [From Gaelic "dark hero"]

Douglas   [From Gaelic "from the black or dark water"]

Doyle   [From Gaelic "dark stranger"]

Duffy   [From the Gaelic "dark-complexioned one"]

Duncan   [From the Gaelic "dark warrior"]

Dusky

Ebony

Espresso

Inky

Jet

Kamaiki [Middle Eastern black coffee]

Keemun [Chinese black tea]

Kerwin [From the Gaelic "little jet black one"]

Layla [Arabic for "dark night"]

Maurice [From the Latin "dark-complexioned"]

Melaine [From the Greek melanos, "black" or "dark"]

Melanin

Malcolm X [Black leader]

Merle [From the Latin "blackbird"]

Midnight [Black cat in introduction of TV's Barnaby Jones]

Mingo [Joel Chandler Harris protagonist]

Morse [From the Old English "son of the dark-complexioned one"]

Nero [Italian for "black, dark"]

Oriole [Beulah's friend in TV series]

Pitch

Pluto [Edgar Allan Poe's "Black Cat"]

Ramoneur [French for "chimney sweep"]

Rufus [Black youth in "The Doonesbury Chronicles"]

Sam [Black cat in "Broomsticks" by Walter de la Mare]

Sapphire [A bluish gem]

Schwartz [German for "black"]

Smoky

Swarthy

Tuxedo

Velvet

Velveteen

Webster [Black cat in "The Story of Webster" by Wodehouse]

BROWNISH

Bordeaux

Bronson [From the Old English "son of the brown one"]

Brownie [Name of the world's richest cat]

Brunella [From the Old French "brown-haired"]

Bruno [Italian for "brown"]

Café [French for "coffee"]

Chestnut

Choc [Chocolate]

Chocolate

Coffee

Cocoa

Cordovan

Creole

Duncan [From the Gaelic "brown warrior"]

Java

Kafeo [Greek for "coffee"]

Khavi [Finnish and Dutch for "coffee"]

Kringle [Scandinavian cookie]

Mahogany

Merida [Brown]

Mocha

Moreno [Spanish for "brown"]

Olive

Orsola [Spanish and Italian for "Ursula"]

Sienna

Tannie [Butterscotch brownie]

Tosca [Fried cookies from Scandinavia]

Ursula [From the Latin "Ursa," "a she-bear"]

GRAYISH

Argenta [Latin for "silvery one"]

Casco [Algonquin for "muddy"]

Dusky

Graham [From the Old English "from the gray land"]

Greely [From the Old English "from the gray meadow"]

Grigio [Italian for "gray"]

Griselda [Teutonic for "gray heroine"]

Griswald [Old German for "from the gray forest"]

Horton [From the Old English "from the gray estate"]

Lloyd [From the Old Welsh "gray-haired one"]

Murky

Shubuta [Choctaw for "smoky"]

Smog

REDDISH

Akako [Japanese for "red"]

Alani [Hawaiian for "orange"]

Amber

Brigit [Celtic goddess with flame-colored hair]

Carambole [Red ball in billiards]

Cardinal

Carmen

Carmine

Carrots

Cerise [French for "cherry"]

Coral

Corcoran [From the Gaelic "of ruddy complexion"]

Flynn [From the Gaelic "son of the red-haired man"]

Frazer [From the Old French "Strawberry"]

Garnet

Ginger

Griffith [Celtic for "red-haired"; var.: Rufus]

Indio [Spanish for "Indian"]

La Roux   [French for "red-head"]

Magenta

Marigold

Muleta   [Bullfighter's red flag]

Naranja   [Spanish for "orange"]

Nectarine

Paprika

Peach

Petunia

Pink Lady   [Mixed drink]

Pink Panther

Pinky

Poinsettia

Pompeii

Poppy

Radcliff   [Old English for "dweller at the red cliff"]

Redcoat

Reddy

Redford   ["From the red ford"]

Rhoda   [Greek for "rose"]

Rojo   [Spanish for "red"]

Rooney   [From the Gaelic "red one"]

Rorky   [From the Gaelic "red king"]

Rory   [Celtic for "ruddy"]

Rosa

Rosado [Portuguese for "rose"]

Rosalie

Rose [Or Rosé]

Rosetta [Italian for "little rose"]

Rosette [French]

Rosie

Rosita [Spanish]

Roslin [From the Old French "little red-haired one"]

Rosso [Italian for "red"]

Rouge [French for "red"]

Roy [Celtic for "red-haired"]

Rozella

Rubia

Rubina

Rubric

Ruby

Ruff [From the French "red-haired"]

Rufina [Fem. form of Rufus]

Rufus [Latin for "red-haired"]

Ruskin [From the Franco-German "little red-head"]

Russell [From the Old French "red-haired"]

Rusty

Rutledge [From the Old English "from the red pool"]

Scarlet

Sherry   [Wine]

Strawberry

Tangerine

Tinto   [Portuguese for "red" and Spanish for "deep-colored"]

Titian

YELLOWISH

Alva   [Latin for "blonde one"]

Amarillo   [Spanish for "yellow"]

Amber

Bellanca   [Italian for "blonde one"]

Blondie

Boyd   [From the Gaelic "blond one"]

Capella   [A brilliant yellow star]

Caramel

Champagne

Citron

Cornelia   [Latin for "yellowish"; var.: Nelli, Cornela]

Crocus

Doré   [From the French "golden-haired"]

Flavian   [Latin for "fair" or "blond"]

Flavius   [Latin for "golden hair"]

Fulvia   [From Latin "golden-haired"]

Gilda   [From the Old English gyldan, "covered with gold"]

Ginger   [Yellow cat in "Ginger and Pickles" by Beatrix Potter]

Golda

Gold Coin

Goldenrod

Goldie

Goldilocks

Lemon

Lemonade

Morela   [Polish for "apricot"]

Oralia   [From the Latin aurelia, "golden"]

Oriana   [Latin for "golden"]

Oro   [Italian and Spanish for "gold"]

Primrose

Saffron

Sandy

Sunflower

Topaz

Yella

Yeller

WHITISH

Alabaster

Albatross

Akasma   [Turkish for "white rose"]

Albinia   [Latin for "white" or "blond"]

Alkali

Ananose   [Indian for "white fawn"]

Argenta   [From the Latin "silvery"]

Ariana   [From the Welsh "silvery"]

Baron   [Movie actor Tom Tyler's white horse]

Bianca, Bianco   [Italian for "white"]

Bip   [White-faced mute created by mime Marcel Marceau]

Blanche   [French for "white"]

Blanco   [Portuguese and Spanish for "white"]

Blinnie   [Irish for "white"]

Candice   [Latin for "glowing white"]

Candida   [Latin for "bright white"]

Chablis

Fadda   [White mule of Mohammed]

Fenella   [From the Gaelic "white-shouldered one"]

Finley   [From the Gaelic "fair-haired valorous one"]

Fiona   [From the Celtic "white"]

Galina   [Russian for "light"]

Gardenia

Genevieve   [Old German for "white wave"]

Gina   [Japanese for "silvery"]

Irving   [From the Old Welsh "white river"]

Ivory

Jack Frost

Jemima [Hebrew for "dove"]

Kenyon [From the Gaelic "white-headed"]

Kimba [The white lion, TV cartoon]

Kira [Fair-haired girl in The Dark Crystal]

Kiska [From the Russian "pure," as in Katerina]

Milky

Morgan [From the Old Welsh "white sea"]

Paleface

Paloma [Spanish for "white dove"]

Pearly

Popcorn

Ricotta

Sherlock [From the Old English "white-haired"]

Siberia

Silver [Horse of the Lone Ranger]

Snowball

Snowdrop [White cat in Through the Looking Glass]

Snowflake

Snow Queen [Heroine of Hans Christian Andersen's tale]

Snow White

Snowy

Sterling [Silver]

Sylvaner [White wine]

Tiza [Spanish for "chalk"]

Trebbiano   [White wine]

Weiss   [German for "white"]

Whitney   [Anglo-Saxon for "from a white island"]

Yelena   [Russian for "lily flower"]

Yeti   [The Abominable Snowman of Tibet]

OTHER COLORS, SHADES, PATTERNS, TEXTURES

Alpaca   [Close-textured fabric]

Angora

Aralac   [A synthetic fiber]

Argyll

Baku   [Dull-finished fiber of buri palm]

Bangkok   [Fine straw used for hats]

Batik

Batiste   [Fine, plain-woven fabric]

Bengaline   [Crosswise-ribbed fabric]

Blueberry

Brilliantine   [Glossy fabric]

Brocade

Calico

Carpincho   [Smooth skin fabric]

Chambray   [Lightweight gingham with a mottled effect]

Chamois

Chantilly   [Lace]

Checkers

Cheviot   [Coarse woolen fabric]

Chiffon

Chino

Chintz

Crinoline

Dobby   [Small-patterned weave]

Georgette

Gingham

Gossamer

Grandelle   [Variety of colors]

Iris   [Greek for "rainbow"]

Jipijapa   [Straw used for Panama hats]

Khaki

Lamé

Leno   [Open-weave fabric]

Mackintosh

Madras

Merino   [Fine wool]

Mixie

Moiré   [Cloth with a wavy pattern]

Morocco   [Fine leather with a pebbled grain]

OD   [Olive drab]

Organdy

Paisley

Percaline [Moiréd cotton]

Pinto

Plum

Poplin

Rainbow

Rayado [Spanish for "streaked"]

Satin

Saxony [Fine woolen fabric]

Shantung [Nubby silk fabric]

Silky

Spotty

Streaky

Stripes

Suede

Surah [Twilled silk]

Tabaret [Striped upholstery fabric]

Tabby

Taffeta

Tartan

Tattersall [Overcheck pattern]

Terry

Twill

Velour

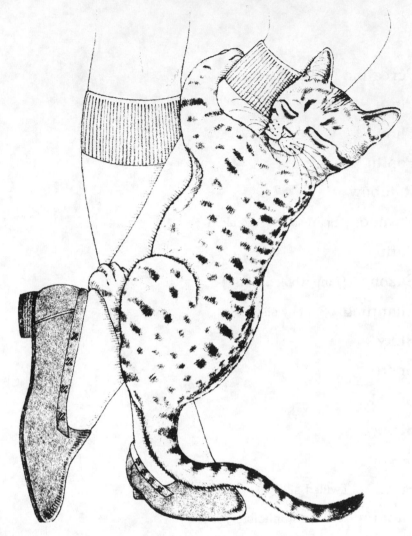

The Sidekick

The Sidekick is known for its fierce loyalty. Glued to your side, it goes where you go—to your bed, kitchen, attic, basement, favorite restaurant, office or bathroom. If you go around in circles, it will follow you round and round. When you stop walking, it will stop too.

Should you leave home and want to make the Sidekick stay, be sure all escape hatches are securely fastened. Shut your doors and windows, lower your louvers, seal off your water pipes, lock your fireplace dampers, and lower the lid of your toilet seat.

Acacia   [Gum arabic]

Accanto   [Italian for "beside, near"]

Adam

Addendum

Alek   [Russian for "helper of mankind"]

Alexandra   [Greek for "helper of mankind"]

Alfreda   [Old English for "elf counselor"]

Alter Ego

Alvin   [From the Old German "friend of all"]

Amasa   [Hebrew for "burden bearer"]

Amelia   [Gothic for "industrious one"; var.: Emelita, Amy, Emmy]

Amica   [Italian for "friend"]

Amico   [Italian for "friendly"]

Amigo   [Spanish for "friend"]

Amity   [Latin, Old French for "friendship"]

Annex

Arbutus   [Climbing plant]

Billy   [Sherlock Holmes's young helper]

Boo Boo   [Yogi Bear's sidekick]

Braccetto   [Italian for "arm-in-arm"]

Bud

Buddy

Bunkie

Certo   [Italian for "certain"]

Chummy

Combo

Creeper   [Climbing plant]

Desma   [Greek for "bond"]

Dexter   [Latin for "right-sided"]

Dillon   [From the Gaelic "faithful one"]

Domovoi   [Russian spirit helpful around the house at night]

Emeline   [From the Teutonic "industrious"]

Ezra   [Hebrew for "helper"]

Fidel   [From the Latin fidelis, "faithful, sincere"; var.: Fidele]

Flankie

Flunky

Friday   [Robinson Crusoe's servant]

G6   [Abbreviation used by the Army for Psychological Warfare and Public Relations]

Gallagher   [From the Gaelic "eager helper"]

Godwin   [Old English for "divine friend"]

Gummy

Hazel   [Housekeeper in a cartoon series]

Hestia   [Goddess of the heart in Greek mythology]

Honeysuckle   [Climbing plant]

Ivy

Jasmine   [Climbing plant]

Konstantinos   [Greek name meaning "firm and constant"]

Krazy Glue

Levi [From the Hebrew "united"]

Marvin [From the Old English "famous friend"]

Mon Ami [French for "my friend"]

Ombra [Italian for "shadow"]

Ophelia [From the Greek "help"; var.: Ofelia, Phelia]

Pard

Polly

PR [Public Relations]

Prentice [From the Middle English "apprentice"]

Próximo [Spanish for "next"]

Putty

Quorum

Roomie [Roommate]

Samantha [Aramaic for "attentive one"]

Sancho Panza [Don Quixote's "esquire"]

Sempre [Italian for "always"]

Snuggle

Thyme [Climbing plant]

Tong [Chinese for "bond"]

Tonto

Toujours [French for "always"]

Vesta [Roman goddess of the household]

Watson [John Watson, Sherlock Holmes's admiring associate]

Wisteria [Climbing plant]

The City Slicker

The City Slicker lives in a high-rise, preferably a luxury apartment. This means that leaping out of windows is not always practical. On the other hand, city living offers plenty of pleasure of its own. There is twenty-four-hour elevator service, so the cat doesn't have to walk up and down the stairs. There are ledges on which to take precarious walks, fire escapes to negotiate, walls to scale, rooftops to leap across, and firemen to summon when it proves to be more difficult coming down than it was going up.

Chadwick   [From Old English "from the warrior's town"]

Cockney   [Native of London's East End]

Cosmo

Cosmopolitan

Elton   [From the Old English "from town"]

Gillie   [Slang for "townsman"]

Melville   [From the Old French "from the industrious one's estate"]

Metro

Metropolis

Milton   [From the Old English "dweller at the mill town"]

Morton   [From the Old English "from the town"; var.: Mort, Mortie]

Newton   [From the Old English "from the new town"]

Norton   [From the Old English "from the north of town"]

Orban   [From the Latin urbane, "born in the city"]

Orville   [From the Old French "from the town"]

Pueblo   [American Indian for "village"]

Rancho   [Spanish for "village"]

Shelton   [From the Old English "from town"]

Sinclair   [From the French "from the town of St. Clair"]

Slicker

Thorpe   [From the Dutch "town"]

Townsend   [From the Old English "from the end of town"]

Townie

Vic   [From the Old French "from the village"]

Walton   [From the Old English "dweller at the forest town"]

Winston   [From the Old English "from a friend's town"]

The Country Bumpkin

The Country Bumpkin enjoys the freedom of country life. It knows it can take off almost any time it wants, cross the street and drop by someone else's home for a milk klatch, or when in the mood keep walking right to the end of town and then some. Long walks, it claims, are good for <u>its</u> health, if not the owner's.

Acorn

Arky   [Slang suggesting "from Arkansas"]

Bartoli   [Spanish for "son of earth." American equivalent for Barth]

Boondocks

Boyce   [From the French "someone who only has rare contact with the town"]

Bruce   [From the Old French "dweller at the thicket"]

Bushua   [Slang for "bushwhacker"]

Campo   [Village square in Italy]

Caspar   [Slang for the unsophisticated]

Chinwhisker

Chump

Dodo

Al Fresco   [Italian for "outdoors"]

Garth   [From the Old Norse "from the garden"]

Garwood   [From the Old English "from the forest"]

George   [From the Latin "land worker, farmer"; var.: Giorgio, Jorge]

Hawley   [From the Old English "from the hedged meadow"]

Haywood   [From the Old English "from the hedged forest"]

Hayseed

Hilton   [From the Old English "from the hill estate"]

Hiram   [Slang for "bumpkin"]

Holbrook   [From the Old English "dweller at the brook in the hollow"]

Holden   [From the Old English "from the depth of the valley"]

Hoosier

Jaboney   [Slang for the unsophisticated]

Jake   [From "country jake"]

Jay

Jeff   [Slang for a Southern "hick"]

Joji   [Japanese for "farmer"]

Kokomo   [Slang for "rustic"]

Lathrop   [From the Old English "from the barns"]

Lennox   [From the Gaelic "abounding in elm trees"]

Lubber

Ludlow   [From the Old English "dweller at the prince's hill"]

Mansfield   [From the Old English "from the field at the river"]

Morley   [From the Old English "from the moor meadow"]

Oakley   [From the Old English "from the oak meadow"]

Ogden   [From the Old English "from the oak valley"]

Rube

Silvanus   [Latin for "dweller of forest"; var.: Silvano, Silvio]

Silvester   [Latin for "from the forest"; var.: Silvestro]

Wakefield   [From the Old English "dweller from the wet field"]

Wampus   [Slang for "lout"]

Yahoo

Yokel   [Var.: Yokey]

Yokum   [Family in the comic strip Li'l Abner]

Yuri   [Dim. of Russian Georgy, "the farmer"]

The Hunter

Hunting comes as naturally to the Hunter as eating or sleeping. After all, among its ancestors was the saber-toothed tiger, whose very presence made other creatures tremble in their hides.

The Hunter is expert at stalking its prey. It has the patience to lie quietly in ambush for hours under the living room couch with an eye fixed on the unfortunate victim. Then, at just the right moment, it pounces upon it in exact imitation of its prehistoric forebears. Its favorite big game are overfed goldfish, Pekingese puppies under two months old, senile canaries, houseplants fewer than ten inches tall, and your big toe poking out under a blanket at night.

Ahab [Whaler captain in Herman Melville's Moby Dick]

Akando [North American Indian name meaning "ambush"]

Artemis [Greek goddess of the hunt]

Bagh [Hindu for "brave"]

Bengal

Chase [From the Old French "to hunt"]

Chaser

Cheetah

Clouseau [Inspector in The Pink Panther]

Diana [Roman goddess of the hunt; var.: Dyanna, Diane]

Huntington [From the Old English "hunter's hill"]

Huntley [From the Old English "from the hunter's meadow"]

Jaguar

Javert [Police inspector in Victor Hugo's Les Misérables]

Leo

Leopard

Mannix [Private eye in TV series]

Orion [Hunter in Greek mythology]

Otis [Greek for "keen-eared"]

Panther

Puma

Tigress

Tigris [Latin for "tiger"]

Uller [Norse god of hunting]

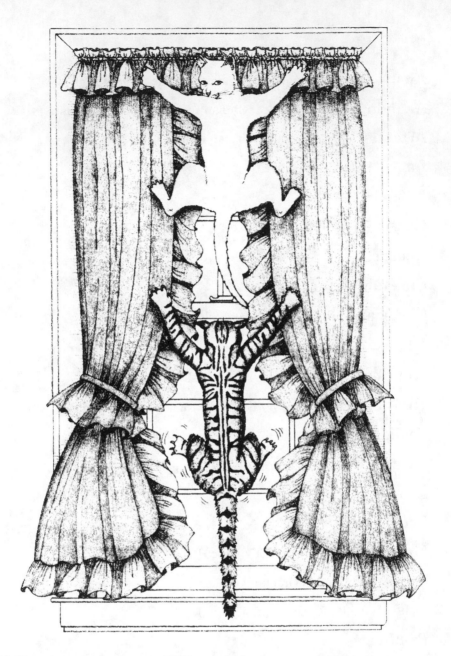

Two of a Kind

Cats often get bored with their human companions, and no wonder. The way cats see it, people have no idea how to have fun;
most of them do not even care to get down on all four to meet

the cat on its own level, and play the game the way it's supposed to be played.

To help the cat cope, many owners keep not one but two cats under the same roof—even though that brings on double the noise, double the scratch marks on the wall, and double the number of cats settling down for the night on the bed. So what? If the home is not large enough for three, perhaps one should leave. The owner, of course.

Abbott and Costello

Abel and Baker   [Chimpanzees sent into orbit in 1959]

Abercrombie and Fitch   [Former store in N.Y.C.]

Adam and Eve

Alpha and Omega

Alphonse and Gaston   [Of "you first" routine]

Amos and Andy

Ann and Andy   [Raggedy]

Antony and Cleopatra

Apples and Oranges

Arnold and Willis   [Two adopted boys on TV's Diff'rent Strokes]

Barnum and Bailey

Beatrice and Benedick   [Caustic wits in Much Ado About Nothing]

Beauty and the Beast

Body and Soul

Bonnie and Clyde

Boswell and Johnson

Brandy and Bitters

Bread and Chocolate

Bubble and Squeak   [Dish of fried cabbage and beef in England]

Cain and Abel

Castor and Pollux

Chapter and Verse

Cheech and Chong

Cheese and Crackers

Chip and Dale

Cloak and Dagger

Coffee and Doughnuts

Corned Beef and Cabbage

Cream and Sugar

Cupid and Psyche

Dante and Beatrice

Daphnis and Chloe   [Shepherd children]

David and Bathsheba

David and Goliath

Ding (and) Dong

Do and Dare

Dun and Bradstreet   [Credit rating agency]

Even (and) Steven

Fame and Fortune

Felix and Oscar   [The Odd Couple]

Flip (and) Flop

Frankie and Johnny   [Legendary lovers]

Franny and Zooey

Fred and Wilma   [The Flintstones]

Fuzzy and Wuzzy   [Nephews of cartoon bear "Barney"]

Gin and Tonic

Ham and Eggs

Hamilton and Burr

Hanky (and) Panky

Hansel and Gretel

Harum (and) Scarum

Head and Shoulders

Heart and Soul

Helen and Paris

Helter (and) Skelter

Hide and Seek

High and Mighty

Hinkey (and) Dinkey   [From a rhyme game]

Humpty (and) Dumpty

Hunky (and) Dory

Ike and Mike

Jack and Jill

Jacob and Leah

Jekyll and Hyde

Jesse and Frank   [James brothers]

Jiggs and Maggie

John and Yoko

Jupiter and Juno

Laurel and Hardy

Laverne and Shirley

Lewis and Clark

Loco (and) Motion

Lone Ranger and Tonto

Macy's and Gimbel's

Mars and Murray   [Candy maker M&M]

Mork and Mindy

Mutt and Jeff

Napoleon and Josephine

Null and Void

On and Off

One and Two

Orlando and Rosalind

Orville and Wilbur   [The Wright brothers]

Part and Parcel

Pen and Ink

Pen and Pencil

Pericles and Aspasia

Peter and Paul

Ping (and) Pong

Pomp and Circumstance

Pork and Beans

Pride and Joy

Pyramus and Thisbe [Play produced by tradesmen within A Midsummer Night's Dream]

Ram and Ron [Basic types of computer information]

Razzle (and) Dazzle

Rock and Roll

Rodgers and Hammerstein

Romeo and Juliet

Romulus and Remus [Founders of ancient Rome]

Rosencrantz and Guildenstern [Characters in Hamlet]

Rough and Tumble

Rum and Coke

Salt and Pepper

Sam and Samantha [The salmon lovers in videogame Samantha]

Scylla and Charybdis

Sears and Roebuck

Sekhmet and Tefnult [Ancient Egyptian lion goddesses]

Silver and Gold

Simon and Garfunkel

Simon and Schuster

Stars and Stripes

Starsky and Hutch

Stout and Ale

Systole and Diastole

Teeter (and) Totter

Tick (and) Tock

Tip (and) Top

Tittle (and) Tattle

To and Fro

Tom and Jerry

Topsy (and) Turvy

Trick (and) Treat

Tristan and Isolde

Tutti (and) Frutti

Tweedledum and Tweedledee

Twiddle (and) Twaddle

Twist and Turn

Up and Down

Valentine and Proteus   [Two Gentlemen of Verona]

Venus and Adonis

Vice (and) Versa

Wash and Wear

Whiskey and Soda

Wild and Woolly

William and Mary

Yin and Yang

A Star Is Born

Sky-gazing is a common preoccupation of cats. Just what intrigues them up there is anybody's guess. It could be the resemblance between the moon and a wheel of cheese, between the

Milky Way and spilled milk, or between a falling star and a bird swooping down. Or perhaps they imagine a distant planet with promise for extra-terrestrial life. This last possibility holds a special fascination for cats: surely any humanoid from outer space could only be an improvement over what's available down here.

Astra   [Greek for "star"]

Celeste   [Latin for "heavenly"; var.: Celesta, Celestine]

Comet

Cometa   [Italian for "comet"]

Cosmos

Domingo   [Spanish for "born on Sunday"]

Dominic   [Latin for "born on Sunday"]

Estelle   [From the Latin "star"; var.: Estella, Stella]

Esther   [Hebrew for "star"]

Gamma   [Ray that lies beyond the electromagnetic spectrum]

Hester   [Persian for "star"]

Meteor

Nadir   [The lowest point]

Nebula   [A cloudlike luminous or dark mass of dust and gases]

Nova   [Variable star]

Olympia   [Greek for "one from heaven"]

Pulsar   [Neutron star]

Quasar   [Quasi-stellar object]

Siderea   [Spanish for "related to the stars"]

Torra   [Deified earth in Roman mythology]

ASTROLOGERS AND ASTRONOMERS

Apollonius [Greek astrologer and mathematician]

Berosos [Babylonian priest]

Bruno [Italian scholar of Hermetic writings]

Copernicus [Polish astronomer]

Galileo [Italian astronomer]

Heraclitus [Greek philosopher who linked the soul with the cosmos for the first time]

Hipparchus [Greek astronomer who first noticed the procession of the equinoxes]

Kepler [German astronomer who placed planets in elliptical orbits]

Morin [French astrologer]

Nostradamus [French astrologer and prophet]

Philolaus [Greek astronomer and numerologist]

CONSTELLATIONS

Andromeda [The Chained Lady] **Cetus** [The Whale]

Antlia [The Air Pump] **Circinus** [The Compasses]

Apus [The Bird of Paradise] **Corvus** [The Crow]

Aquila [The Eagle] **Dorado** [The Swordfish]

Ara [The Altar] **Fornax** [The Furnace]

Argo [Ship] **Grus** [The Crane]

Auriga [The Charioteer] **Hydra** [The Sea Serpent]

Carina [The Keel] **Lacerta** [The Lizard]

Cassiopeia [Cassiopeia's Chair] **Lupus** [The Wolf]

Cepheus [The Monarch] **Musca** [The Fly]

Norma [The Rule]   Perseus [The Rescuer]

Octans [The Octant]   Puppis [The Stern]

Orion [The Hunter]   Sagittarius [The Archer]

Pavo [The Peacock]   Vela [The Sail]

Pegasus [The Winged Horse]   Vulpecula [The Little Fox]

MOON DEITIES

Artemis [Greek]   Hecate [Greek]

Cynthia [Greek]   Phoebe [Greek]

Diana [Roman]   Selene [Greek]

SUN DEITIES

Apollo [Greek]   Shanas [Semitic]

Helios [Greek]   Sol [Roman]

Phoebus [Greek]   Surya [Hindu]

Ra [Egyptian]   Titan [Greek]

Samitar [Hindu]   Utu [Sumerian]

CHALDEAN NAMES FOR PLANETS
(ANCIENT BABYLONIA)

Ishtar [Venus]   Nerval [Mars]

Marduk [Jupiter]   Ninurta [Saturn]

Nabu [Mercury]

PLANETS

Ceres [Minor]	Mercury	Saturn
Juno [Minor]	Neptune	Uranus
Jupiter	Pallas [Minor]	Venus
Mars	Pluto	Vesta [Minor]

STARS

Aldebaran	Canicula	Deneb
Antares	Canopus	Polaris
Betelgeuse	Capella	Sirius
		Vega

ASTROLOGICAL SIGNS

Aries [March 21–April 19]

Taurus [April 20–May 20]

Gemini [May 21–June 20]

Cancer [June 21–July 22]

Leo [July 23–August 22]

Virgo [August 23–September 22]

Libra [September 23–October 22]

Scorpio [October 23–November 21]

Sagittarius [November 22–December 21]

Capricorn [December 22–January 19]

Aquarius [January 20–February 18]

Pisces [February 19–March 20]

The More the Merrier

Some cat owners never learn to say "Enough already." Their doors are always open to any cat looking for a handout, and that usually means every cat in the neighborhood, stray or not. Word travels fast in cat circles, especially when the subject is food.

Multiple cat owners must learn how to dole out favors to each of their cats, lest they appear to play favorites and cause discord among the rank and file. It's important that each cat has its own dish (with its name clearly imprinted on it) — even though as things turn out they all will share the same dish (yours) at dinner time—and that each has its own sleeping accommodations, even though they will all end up in the same bed (yours) at night.

THREESOMES

A, B, C

Athos, Porthos, Aramis [The Three Musketeers]

Bell, Book, and Candle

Bobbie Jo, Billie Jo, Betty Jo [Sisters in TV's Petticoat Junction]

Caspar, Melchior, Balthasar [The Magi]

Character, Capacity, Credit [Financial code for credit worthiness]

Faith, Hope, Charity

Farragut, Enterprise, Republic [United Federation vessels in Star Trek]

Fatso, Fusso, Lazo [Ghosts in comic Caspar, the Friendly Ghost]

Fidelity, Bravery, Integrity [FBI's motto]

Jerry, James, John [Brothers in nursery rhyme "The Three Sons"]

Lachesis, Clotho, Atropos [The Fates]

Larry, Moe, Curly [The Three Stooges]

Lock, Stock, Barrel

Louie, Dewey, Huey [Donald Duck's nephews]

166

Marie, Toulouse, Berlioz [The cats in The Aristocats]

Maurice, Barry, Robin [The Bee Gees]

Mistress Flora, Mistress Fauna, Mistress Merrywhether [Good fairies]

Melvin, Alfred, David [Initials that inspired the magazine title MAD]

Snap, Crackle, Pop

Tic, Tac, Toe

Tom, Dick, Harry

Wendy, Michael, John [The Darling children in Peter Pan]

Yum-Yum, Peep-Bo, Pitti-Sing [Little maids in The Mikado]

FOURSOMES

Dominick, Marcus, Felipe, Restivo [Sons of King Frederick and Queen Christina in videogame Warlords]

Inky, Blinky, Pinky, Clyde [Devouring monsters in Pac-Man]

Jo, Meg, Beth, Amy [Sisters in Little Women by Louisa May Alcott]

John, Paul, George, Ringo [The Beatles]

Matthew, Mark, Luke, John [Gospels]

Peepeye, Pipeye, Poopeye, Pupeye [Popeye's nephews]

Shadow, Speedy, Bashful, Pokey [Ghostlike monsters in Pac-Man: red, pink, blue, orange]

Swords, Wands, Cups, Pentacles [Suits in Tarot cards]

FIVESOMES

Blossom, Frilly, Violet, Milly, Thumper [Rabbit children in Bambi]

Eugene, Steve, Daisy, Helen, Ben, Luke [Children in Look Homeward, Angel]

Rupa, Vedana, Sanjna, Sanskara, Vignana [The skandhas, or psychological components, in Tibetan Buddhism: form, feeling, perception, concept, consciousness]

Wummings, Hearn, Croft, Martinez, Wilson [Platoon members in The Naked and the Dead by Norman Mailer]

SIXSOMES

Grover, Bert, Sherlock Hemlock, Cookie Monster, Ernie, Roosevelt Franklin [Muppets]

Peyo, Jokey, Greedy, Clumsy, Grouchy, Smurfet [The Smurf family]

Smith, Johnson, Williams, Jones, Brown, Miller [Most common names in the U.S.]

Who, What, When, Where, Why, How [Reporter's questions]

SEVENSOMES

Atman, Manas, Buddhi, Prana, Linga Sharira, Shutla Sharira, Kama [Principles of Man, according to Hindu theosophy: spirit, mind, soul, vital force, astral body, physical body, principle of desire]

Aventine, Caelia, Capitoline, Esquiline, Palatine, Quirinal, Viminal [Hills of Rome]

Bias, Chilon, Cleobulus, Periander, Pittacus, Solon, Thales [Sages of Greece]

Dopey, Sneezy, Happy, Grumpy, Doc, Bashful, Sleepy [The dwarfs in "Snow White"]

Muladhara, Swadisthana, Manipura, Anahata, Vishuddki, Ajna, Sahasrara [Chakras, or energy centers, in Tantra and Kundalini Yoga]

Pride, Envy, Anger, Sloth, Avarice, Prodigality, Gluttony, Lust   [The Seven Deadly Sins]

Sunday, Monday, Tuesday, Wednesday, Thursday, Friday, Saturday

MISCELLANEOUS

[Apostles]:

Andrew	Judas	Simon
Bartholomew	Matthew	Thaddeus
James	Peter	Thomas
John	Philip	

[Apples]:

Baldwin	Gano	Oldenburg
Belmont	Ingram	Rambo
Benoni	Jonathan	Seckel
Collins	Lodi	Spitzenberg
Cortland	Louise	Sutton
Duchess	McIntosh	

[Archangels]:

Abdiel	Jophiel	Uriel
Chamuel	Michael	Zadkiel
Gabriel	Raphael	

[Berries]:

Blackberry	Dewberry	Loganberry
Blueberry	Gooseberry	Mulberry
Boysenberry	Huckleberry	Raspberry
Cranberry	Juneberry	Strawberry

[Bible Characters]:

Aaron	Belshazzar	Elisha
Adam	Benjamin	Eve
Ahab	Cain	Ezekiel
Abraham	Daniel	Gideon
Absalom	David	Goliath
Barnabas	Delilah	Hagar
Bathsheba	Elijah	Herod

Hezekiah Micah Ruth
Jacob Miriam Samson
Jesse Moses Samuel
Jezebel Noah Sarah
Jonah Naomi Shadrah
Joseph Nicodemus Silas
Joshua Onan Simon
Judas Paul Solomon
Lazarus Peter Thomas
Martha Rachel Timothy
Matthew Rebekah Zedekiah

[Coiffures]:

Bangs Marcel Ringlets
Bob Pigtails Shaggy
Chignon Pompadour Swirl
Cowlick Ponytail Tonsure
Frizz Puffs

[Coins]:

Bolivar Krona Ruble
Dinar Lira Rupee
Drachma Mark Won
Escudo Nickel Yen
Franc Peseta
Florin Peso

[Furniture styles]:

Adams Florentine Sheraton
Biedermeier Heppelwhite Tudor
Chippendale Mission Wicker
Directoire Queen Anne Windsor
Duncan Phyfe Regency

[Insect names created by the Indian tribe Miwoks]: Hesutu [lifting a yellow jacket's nest from the earth], Momusu [yellow jackets gathered into a pile during winter], Muata [yellow jackets in the nest], Nokonyu [katydid's nose just above its mouth], Timu [black and white caterpillar emerging from the ground]

[Evil knights of King Arthur's Round Table]:

Andred	King Mark	Pinell
Damas	Meleagrance	Turquire
Gringamore	Mordred	
Helius	Phelot	

[Good knights of King Arthur's Round Table]:

Abbellius	Dinadan	Melias
Alisander	Ebel	Naram
Balin	Epinogris	Percivale
Bedicere	Floridas	Persides
Berel	Galagers	Sadok
Caradoc	Gilmere	Sorlons
Clegis	Lionel	Ulfius
Darras	Managgan	Wisshard

[Months]:

January	May	September
February	June	October
March	July	November
April	August	December

[Months—derivations of names]:

Janus	Malus	Septem
Februarius	Junius	Octo
Mars	Julius	Novem
Apru	Augustus	Decem

[Muses]: Calliope [epic poetry], Clio [history], Erato [love poetry], Euterpe [lyric poetry], Melpomene [tragedy], Polyhymnia [song and oratory], Terpsichore [dancing and choral song], Thalia [comedy and burlesque], Urania [astronomy]

[Phonetic alphabet (words used in voice transmission over radio)]:

Alpha	Golf	Mike
Bravo	Hotel	November
Charlie	India	Oscar
Delta	Juliet	Papa
Echo	Kilo	Quebec
Foxtrot	Lima	Romeo

Sierra	Victor	Yankee
Tango	Whiskey	Zulu
Uniform	X-ray	

[Characters in the Robin Hood story]:

Allan-a-Dale	Maid Marian	Sheriff of
Friar Tuck	Prince John	Nottingham
Little John	Robin Hood	Will Scarlet

[Roman gods]:

Ceres	Mars	Venus
Diana	Mercury	Vesta
Juno	Minerva	Vulcan
Jupiter	Neptune	

[Sha Na Na]:

Bowser	Donny	Lennie
Chico	Jocko	Screamin'
Denny	Johnny	

The Social Lion

The Social Lion has an aristocratic bloodline—or so it thinks. With its head held high, this cat exudes confidence as it makes its way from one garbage dump to another. Even its meow has class, a sort of British twang to it.

Conscious of its noble ancestry, the Social Lion is choosy about its feline friends. It checks them out carefully, one by one, making sure they live in the right part of town, move in the right circles, have traveled widely, and eat only the finest of leftovers.

173

Acapulco

Astor

Beau Monde

Bergdorf

Bloomingdale

Bon Ton

Bonwit

Cartier

Cassini

Chapeau

Chichi

Cornelius

Deb

Du Pont

Duchess

Duke

Fairbanks

Gucci

Lady Di

Ladyship

Limo

Lordship

Mark Cross

Mayfair

Mayflower

Montgomery   [From the Old French "from the wealthy one's hill"]

Morgan

Nobby

Nobilis   [Latin for "noble"]

Nolan   [From the Gaelic "famous"]

Otto   [Old German for "the rich one"]

Pierpont

Rico   [Spanish for "rich"]

Ritzy

Rockefeller

Rothschild

Saratoga

Señor   [Spanish for "sir"]

Signor   [Italian for "sir"]

Silk-Stocking

Sotheby

Tiffany

Tony

Tuxedo

Ultra

Vanderbilt

Von Furstenburg

Windsor

The Showpiece

A quick peek in the mirror first thing every morning is enough to confirm what the Showpiece has suspected all along—that it is a ravishing creature. Everyone says so. Owners take inordinate pride in their Showpiece, describing its good looks every chance they get. Usually this is within earshot of the cat, who already knows all that but likes to hear it over and over nevertheless.

Adah [Hebrew for "tiara," "ornament"]

Adina [From Hebrew "graceful, delicate"]

Adonia [Greek for "beautiful"]

Ah Kum [Chinese for "good as gold"]

Anne [Hebrew for "graceful one"; var.: Nita, Nina, Anita, Nanette, Anna]

Antonia [Latin for "priceless"; var.: Toni, Netty]

Aphrodite [Greek goddess of love and beauty]

Atractivo [Spanish for "attractive"]

Aurora [Latin for "dawn"]

Becky [Becky Sharp, the entrancing beauty in Vanity Fair]

Belinda [Old Spanish for "pretty"; var.: Belle, Belvia]

Belle [French for "beautiful"]

Belleza [Italian for "beauty"]

Bello [Italian and Spanish for "beautiful"]

Blossom

Bonita [Spanish for "pretty"; var.: Bonnie, Bonny, Nita]

Cara [Italian for "dear"]

Champagne

Charlie

Cinderella

Cleopatra

176

Couronne [French for "crown"]

Donato [From the Latin "a gift"]

Dorinda [Spanish for "beautiful gift"]

Ducky

Frilly

Garbo

Hedy [Lamar]

Helga [From the Teutonic "holy"]

Hepzibah [Seductive skunk in comic strip Pogo]

Juno [Jupiter's wife, queen of the Roman gods]

Kasper [Persian for "precious stone"]

Kate [Greek for "pure"]

Katy

La-di-da

Lawrence [From the Latin "laurel-crowned one"; var.: Larry Lorenz, Lorenzo]

Majesta [Latin for "majestic one"]

Marilyn [Monroe]

Marv [Short for "marvelous"]

Matthew [From the Hebrew "gift of God"]

Maximilian [From the Latin "epitome of perfection"; var.: Maxie, Maxim, Maximo]

Mona Lisa

Narcissus

Nora [Pretty wife of Torwald Helmer in Ibsen's A Doll's House]

Olaf   [From Old Norse "old relic"; five Norwegian kings were named Olaf]

Osmar   [From the Old English "divinely glorious"]

Pandora   [Greek for "all gifted"]

Pippin

Queenie   [From the Teutonic "queen"; var.: Queena]

Regina   [Italian for "queen"]

Roxana   [Persian for "brilliant one"]

Snazzy

Spiffy

Tallulah   [Bankhead]

The Face   [Nickname of actress Anita Colby]

Vanity

Vashti   [Persian for "beautiful one"]

DIAMONDS OF FAME

Cullinan

Kohinoor

Lesotho

Punch Jones

Sancy

FLOWERS

Common Names

Azalea	Bluebell	Canna
Begonia	Camellia	Carnation

Columbine	Hyacinth	Peony
Crocus	Jasmine	Petunia
Daffodil	Lavender	Poppy
Dahlia	Lilac	Sweetpea
Daisy	Lily	Violet
Gardenia	Marigold	Wisteria
Gladiolus	Pansy	Zinnia

Botanical Names

Arabis [Rock cress]	Narcissus [Daffodil]
Bellis [Daisy]	Papaver [Poppy]
Campanula [Bellflower]	Scilla [Bluebell]
Erica [Heath]	Solidago [Goldenrod]
Hedera [Ivy]	Viola [Pansy]

GEMS

Agate	Emerald	Pearl
Amber	Jade	Rhinestone
Beryl	Jasper	Ruby
Crystal	Onyx	Sapphire
Diamond	Opal	Topaz

GEM CUTS

| Briolette | Kohinoor | Pendeloque |
| Cabochon | Marquise | Regent |

Life of the Party

This cat not only tolerates but actually enjoys the company of people. In fact, its performance improves with the size of the audience.

Gregarious by nature, at a party this cat will join conversations on almost any topic, leap from one lap to another regardless of distance, and peck everyone on the cheek with its sticky little nose and rough little tongue. Its favorite spot is the buffet table. Here in between drinks it will entertain its taste buds with bites of your Filet of Sole Amandine, Spinach Salad, Orange Chiffon Cake, and candlesticks.

Abigail [From the Hebrew "source of joy"; var.: Abbie, Abby]

Alice [Female bartender in Andy Capp comic strip]

Alvita [From the Latin "vivacious"]

Anastasia [Greek for "of the resurrection"; var.: Stacy, Stacia]

Bacchanal [A drunken reveler]

Bacchus [Roman god of wine and festivities]

Bon Vivant

Bravo

Bubbles

Busybody

Caper

Carnie

Carousal

Confetti

Dynamo

Felicia [Latin for "happy one"]

Feste [Fool in Twelfth Night]

Fiesta

Fracas

Happy

Harum-Scarum

Hilary   [From the Latin "hilarius"; var.: Hilario]

Hooligan

Hoopla

Houdini

Huggermugger

Jazzy

Jeepers

Jolly

Klutz

Lollapalooza

Lucy   [From the Latin lucia, "bringer of light"]

Maraca

Nifty

Obie   [Award for outstanding theatrical performance]

Peperone   [Italian for "pepper"]

Pepita

Pepper

Peppy

Perky

Picnic

Poppy   [Intoxicating flower]

Razzle-Dazzle

Razzmatazz

Ruckus

Rumpus

Saturnalia   [Occasion or period of unrestrained revelry and licentiousness]

Saucy

Schnapps   [Any of various strong liquors]

Snoopy

Spicy

Sport

Sprite   [An elfish person; a disembodied spirit]

Sunshine

Tiger

Trickster

Trump

Wacko

Whoopee

Zowie

SPICES

Caraway	Coriander	Oregano
Cardamom	Curry	Saffron
Cassia	Ginger	Sassafras
Cayenne	Juniper	Tarragon
Chili	Marjoram	Vanilla
Cinnamon	Nutmeg	

CARD GAMES

Baccarat	Écarté	Lotto
Bezique	Faro	Monte
Bluff	Gin	Pinochle
Canasta	Gobang	Poker
Casino	Keno	Rummy
		Whist

FAMOUS GAMBLING PLACES

Calcutta	Las Vegas	Reno
Copacabaña	Monte Carlo	

MISCELLANEOUS GAMES

Acey-Deucy	Jigsaw
Bagatelle	Mah-Jongg
Bingo	Ouija
Blackjack	Parcheesi
Charades	Roulette
Checkers	Scrabble
Dice	Skat
Dominoes	Snooker
Hopscotch	Wingo

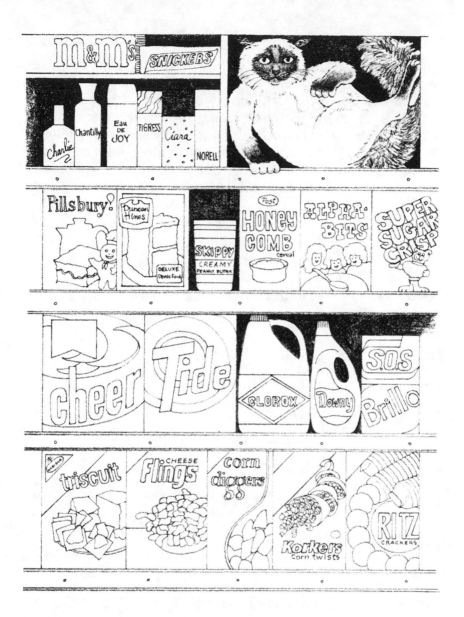

The Logotype

This cat wants to be a household word. So why not borrow a name already well established at someone else's expense?

Like all cats, the Logotype is happier if the name suits its personality, such as it may be. Perfumes and toiletries please the dainty types. Those with a bubbly disposition go for soda pop. The well-groomed have an affinity for cleaners and detergents. Cereals go over big with cats who get up with the rest of the family in the morning. Candy names please the sugary types. Imbibers identify themselves with famous liquor brands. Those with a sweet tooth like the names of cakes, pies, puddings, and ice cream, while the few who actually chew their food as opposed to swallowing it whole look to cookies, crackers, chips, and chewing gum for inspiration.

TOILETRIES

Activa	Crazy Baby	Mary Kay
Adorn	Cuticura	Maxi
Afta	Dainty Miss	Nivea
Angel Face	Dippity Do	Summer Blond
Aquaphor	Dry Guy	Tip-Top
Arrid	Happy Face	Toni
Avallo	Hot Stuff	
Coty	Loving Care	

PERFUMES AND COLOGNES

Adolfo	Chanel	Enjoli
Ambush	Charles of the Ritz	Flambeau
Aphrodisia	Charlie	Flatterie
Aramis	Chaz	Jovan
Babe	Chevelle	Le Dix
Brut	Chloe	L'Oréal
Casaque	Emilio Pucci	Maja

Mitsouko	Tailspin	White Shoulders
Old Spice	Taji	Wind Song
Ondine	Tigress	Zibeline
Prince Matchabelli	Ultima	Zizanie
Schiaparelli	Vivari	
Tabu	White Mist	

SOFT DRINKS

Coke	Ovaltine	Sprite
Dr. Pepper	Pepsi	Yoo-Hoo
Fresca	Royal Crown	Wink
Hawaiian Punch	Schweppes	
Kool Aid	Seven-Up	

SOAPS AND DETERGENTS

Ajax	Duz	Lux
Camay	Glo-Coat	Mr. Clean
Cascade	Jergens	Top Job
Dove	Lava	Wisk
Downy		

CEREALS

Apple Jack	Cheerios	Frankenberry
Boo Berry	Chex	Kaboom
Captain Crunch	Count Chocula	Pink Panther

Quisp　　　　　　Sugar Pop(s)　　　　Wheatie(s)

Rice Krispie(s)　　Trix

CAKES, PIES, PUDDINGS AND ICE CREAM

Ding Dong(s)　Morton　[Pastry]　Yankee Doodle(s)

Drake('s)　　　Pepperidge　[Farm]　Yodel(s)

Häagen-Dazs　Sara Lee

Jell-O　　　　Tasty Kake

COOKIES, CRACKERS AND CHIPS

Bugle(s)　　　　Cornnut(s)　　　Lorna Doone(s)

Capri　　　　　Doo Dad(s)　　　Milano

Chip-a-Roo(s)　Fling(s)　　　　Oreo

Cocochip(s)　　Frito-Lay　　　　Pringle(s)

CHEWING GUM AND MINTS

Bazooka　　　　Doublemint　　　Tic Tac(s)

Chiclet(s)　　　Dubble Bubble

MEDICINES

Alka-Seltzer　　Bufferin　　　　Miltown

Bromo Seltzer　Librium

CANDY

Baby Ruth　　　Butterfinger　　Choo Choo

Bit-O-Honey　　Caravelle　　　Chuckles

188

Chunky

Cracker Jack(s)

Crunchola

Fluffer Nutter

Ghirardelli

Goober(s)

Jelly Belly

Jinks

Jujube(s)

Jujyfruit

Kit-Kat

Krackel

Krinkel

M&M

Mary Jane

Mello Mint

Milky Way

Necco

Nibs

Nut Loaf

Oh Henry!

Pokie(s)

Raisinet

Snickers

Snow Cap(s)

Sugar Daddy

Sugar-Nut

Tootsie Roll

Twizzler

Zagnut

LIQUOR

Bacardi

Beefeater

Black Velvet

Budweiser

Calvert

Castillo

Chivas Regal

Coors

Cutty Sark

Dewar's

Early Times

Gilbey's

Heublein

Imperial

J&B

Jack Daniel's

Jim Beam

Johnnie Walker

Kahlua

Kamchatka

Kessler

Old Crow

Popov

Schenley

Seagram

Smirnoff

Tanqueray

Ten High

Wolfschmidt

The Sleepyhead

All cats doze off on occasion. Not so the Sleepyhead. This cat dozes all day long.

Now and then, the Sleepyhead will actually get up and move its body to another sleeping spot. This phenomenon is usually referred to as somnambulism, or sleepwalking. Consult a psychiatrist if you are concerned. Perhaps even take your cat with you for your first visit. As long as there is a couch in the doctor's office, the Sleepyhead will be glad to keep you company.

Anesthesia

Anshar   [Babylonian god of darkness and night]

Bostezo   [Spanish for "yawn"]

Cómodo   [Spanish for "comfortable"]

Cushie

Davenport   [Couch]

Divano   [Italian for "couch"]

Frink   [The collapsing creature in Dr. Seuss' Sleep Book]

Godfrey   [Old German for "divinely peaceful"; var.: Golffredo, Godofredo]

Grandall   [Sleepwalking creature in Dr. Seuss' Sleep Book]

Hangover

Hypnos   [Greek god of sleep]

Inertia

Jeffrey   [From the Old French "divinely peaceful"; var.: Godfrey, Jeff]

Jo & Mo   [Champion sleepwalkers in Dr. Seuss' Sleep Book]

Kerplunk

Klunk

Lullaby

McPhail   [Snoring creature in Dr. Seuss' Sleep Book]

Mopy

Morpheus   [Son of Hypnos]

Nappy

Nirvano   [Sleeping gas inhaled by Buck Rogers]

Noah   [Hebrew for "rest, comfort"]

Ozio   [Italian for "idleness"]

Plopper

P.M.

Poop

Riposo   [Italian for "rest"]

Rip Van Winkle

Rockabye

Serena, Sereno   [From the Latin Serenus, "tranquil one"]

Siesta   [Spanish for "nap"]

Slow-poke

Sogno   [Italian for "dream"]

Somnambula, Somnambulo   [Italian for "sleepwalker"]

Somnus   [Roman god of sleep]

Van Vleck   [Sleepy bug in Dr. Seuss' Sleep Book]

Vladimir   [From the Old Slavic "royally peaceful"]

Wilt

Winkie

Yawn

The Complete Nut

The Complete Nut enjoys all types of activities—with or without an audience. It amuses itself by turning backward somersaults in the air, trying to alight on its feet but landing smack on its head. It considers people's legs to be the best scratching post of all; enjoys bounding across the room for no reason at all, knocking over vases supposedly out of its reach; and leaping out of third-story windows to see if it can make it.

Ado

Analgesia

Attivita   [Italian for "activity"]

Attivo   [Italian for "active"]

Azione   [Italian for "action"]

Bananas

Bedlam

Boffo

Boo-boo

Bozo

Cabaret

Caper

Caprice

Cassidy   [From the Irish "clever, ingenious one"]

Clyde   [Orangutan in movie Every Which Way But Loose]

Corky

Crazy Eddie

Cuckoo

Curio

Daffy

Demento

Dodo

Dotty

Dynamo

Faux Pas

Flak

Folly

Frenzy

Gambado   [A prank or antic]

Geronimo

Giddy

Giggle

Glenda   [Anagram for "dangle"]

Goofy

Hippety

Hokum

Hopscotch

Howdy Doody

Hyper

Hysteria

Ignatius   [Latin for "fiery one"]

Jigger

Jimjams   [Jitters]

Jitters

Júbilo   [Spanish for "joy"]

Kiko   [Kangaroo in Paul Terry cartoons]

Mad Hatter

Mania

Murphy's Law

Nerf

Neuro   [Neurotic]

Panic

Paranoia

Pazzo   [Italian for "crazy"]

Phobia

Ping-Pong

Pitapat

Psycho

Smirk

Soma   [Happiness drug in Brave New World]

Sorriso   [Italian for "smile"]

Spiel   [German for "play, game"]

Tate   [From the Middle English "cheerful one"]

Teresa   [Anagram for "teaser"]

Trauma

Vera   [Anagram for "rave"]

Vertigo

Vito   [From the Latin vitus, "alive"]

Vivo   [Italian for "alive"]

Woozy

Baby's Best Friend

This cat loves children—the smaller the better. People do look cute on all fours, better than they do standing up. What's more, a child's own egotistical interests do not yet interfere with what's best for the cat.

Generous to a fault, Baby's Best Friend likes to share everything with the latest addition to the family: the bottle, the pacifier, the baby blanket, all toys—and, above all, the crib, which it considers a vast improvement over beds designed for cats.

Alfred   [From the Old English elf, "counselor"]

Alma   [Latin for "fostering"]

Baby Ben   [Trade name for clocks]

Bailey   [From the Old French "trusted one"; var.: Bayley]

Baldwin   [Old German for "protector"]

Cicerone   [Italian for "guide"]

Corwin   [From the Old English "heart friend"]

Culla   [Italian for "cradle"]

Drew   [From the Teutonic "trustworthy"]

Edmund   [From the Old English "rich protector"]

Edwin   [From the Old English "prosperous friend"; var.: Eddie, Eddy]

Elridge   [German for "mature, older counselor"]

Freya   [Norse goddess of love]

Hector   [From the Greek "steadfast"]

Homer   [From the Greek homeros, "security, pledge"; var.: Omero]

Howard   [From the Old English "chief guardian"]

Marshall   [From the Middle English "attendant to the manor"]

Meredith   [From the Old Welsh "guardian"]

Nanny

Osmond   [From the Old English "divine counselor"]

Philo   [Greek for "loving, friendly"]

Posto   [Italian for "place," "post"]

Proctor   [Latin for "guide and administrator"]

Ramona   [From the Teutonic "wise protectress"; fem. form of Raymond]

Randolph   [From the Old English shield-wolf, a war shield that protected its owner]

Raymond   [From the Old German "wise protector"; var.: Raimondo]

Redmond   [From the Teutonic "counselor"]

Salvador   [Spanish for "savior," one who guides]

Sandra   [Greek for "helper of mankind"]

Teddy

Waite   [From the Middle English "guard, watchman"]

Ward   [From the Old English "guardian"; var.: Warden]

Warren   [From the Old German "watchman"]

Warwick   [From the Old English "fortress of the defender's family"]

Winifred   [From the Teutonic "peaceful friend"; var.: Freddy, Winnie, Winnifred]

Winthrop   [From the Old English "dweller at the friend's place"]

NURSERY CHARACTERS

Bo-Peep

Busy Bee

Cock Robin

Curly Locks

Goldilocks

Jack Frost

Jack Sprat

Little Boy Blue

Miss Muffet

Old King Cole

Peter Piper

Sandman

Wee Willie Winkie

Now You See It,
Now You Don't

All cats have an ability to disappear just when you're most anxious to find them. This is a protective technique they developed thousands of years ago as a way of confusing enemies. The subterfuge worked so well that they've been refining it ever since. Today, they consider it an art to be passed from one generation to the next, with much chuckling.

Of course, the cat can always see you. And hear you. As a matter of fact, it enjoys listening to your voice grow hoarse from trying to establish contact. Just as you have lost your ability to make any sound, the cat will suddenly materialize and pretend it has been just a few feet away all along.

Abel   [From the Hebrew "evanescence"]

Abracadabra

Airlia   [Greek for "ethereal"]

Ammon   [From the Egyptian amen, "the hidden"]

Arcamun   [Latin for "hidden places"]

Armadio   [Italian for "closet"]

Atlantis   [The continent that vanished]

Banshee   [Spirit]

Boomerang

Cabala

Cameo

Capatoza   [Flourish of cape in bullfighting]

Casper   ["The Friendly Ghost"]

Catch-22

Comet

Déjà-Vu

Domovos   [Russian ghost]

Effluvium

Enigma

Ephemeron

Garwor   [Now-you-see-it-now-you-don't predator in videogame Wizard of Oz]

Gustave   [Anagram for "vaguest"]

Houdini

Jack-in-the-box

Magic

Nihility

Nixie   [German water spirit able to become invisible]

Peter Pan

Phantom

Phenomenon

Possum

Ropero   [Spanish for "closet"]

Scuba

Sir Garlon   [The invisible knight of King Arthur's Round Table]

Solaris   [Mysterious plane in science fiction]

Specter

Spook

Streaker

Tania   [Russian fairy queen]

Thorwor   [Now-you-see-it-now-you-don't predator in videogame
   Wizard of Oz]

Tiptoe

Twinkle

Whodunnit

Winky

The Birdwatcher

The Birdwatcher knows its place—the windowsill. Anyone or anything moving in this territory does so at its own peril.

This cat is wise enough to realize that, as a practical matter, watching birds beats chasing them. Looking requires less energy than running all over the place trying to catch critters who can fly. This is not to suggest that the Birdwatcher is a do-nothing. On the contrary. In its dreams it brings down many a bird in one fell swoop. After such grueling dreams, it's no wonder the Birdwatcher is often so completely exhausted.

Argus   [Greek for "watchful, vigilant"]

Audubon

Axel   [From the Old German "father of peace"]

Daphne   [From the Greek "laurel tree"]

Epops   [From the Greek comedy The Birds by Aristophanes]

Falda   [Icelandic for "tucked-under wings"]

Foco   [Spanish for "focus"]

Goggle

Gregory   [From the Latin "watchful one"; var.: Gregor, Gregorio]

Horace   [From the Latin Horatius, "keeper of the hours"; var.: Horatio, Orazio]

Humphrey   [From the Old German "peaceful Hun"]

Ira   [Hebrew for "watchful one"]

Laissez-Faire

Lester   [From the Latin "chosen camp"]

Manatuck   [Algonquin for "look-out place"]

Nydia   [Latin for "nest, refuge"]

Ojo   [Spanish for "eye"]

Palomar   [Famous observatory near Pasadena]

Paparazzo

Paul Pry

Peeping Tom

Pepe   [Anagram for "peep"]

Periscope

Pince-nez   [Type of glasses]

Radar

Rubberneck

Serena   [Latin for "serene"]

Snooper

Solita   [From the Latin "alone"]

Sonar

Spotter

Squint

Theora   [From the Greek "watcher"]

Thoreau

Vigilante

Vista   [Italian for "sight"]

Yerkes   [Famous observatory in Wisconsin]

The Sorehead

Nothing upsets this cat more than losing, or even the very idea
of it. As far as it is concerned, it is not how you play the game,
but whether you win or lose.

Should it come in second—as, for example, in a race to the
dinner table—the Sorehead will let you know how it feels. It will

go to the nearest corner and sulk. Unless the cat is convinced you really mean it, your apology will fall on deaf ears. This is a cat that needs time to sort things out, to see who was right. It will take the Sorehead a few weeks to conclude that when it comes to sportsmanship, never trust people.

Aceto   [Italian for "vinegar"]

Acido   [Italian for "sour"]

Amaro   [Italian for "sour"]

Amargo   [Spanish for "bitter"]

Angst   [German for "anxiety"]

Animus   [Latin for "animosity"]

Azami   [Japanese for "thistle flower," symbol of a surly temper]

Boohoo

Dolore   [Italian for "pain"]

Dolores   [Spanish for "sorrows"; var.: Dolly, Doloria, Lola, Lolita, Lolly]

Dolorosa   [Italian for "dolorous"]

Doreen   [From the Gaelic "sullen one"]

Dumps

Excedrin

Grouser

Grover   [Of <u>Sesame Street</u> fame]

Grumpy

Maddie

Mona   [Anagram for "moan"]

Mopy

Oscar   ["Oscar the Grouch" of Sesame Street]

Petula   [From the Latin "peevish"; var.: Petulia]

Pickle

Pill

Rebel

Rimorso   [Italian for "remorse"]

Rose   [Anagram for "sore"]

Sourpuss

Sulky Sue

Trista   [From the Latin "melancholic"]

Vinegar

The Supercat

This cat will join you in reading the funnies—looking over the panels one by one, snickering to itself—because it identifies with the comic-strip heroes. As far as the Supercat is concerned, there is nothing far-fetched about the antics of superheroes. Flying through space, penetrating walls, vanquishing enemies, and vanishing into thin air? It's all in a day's work for the Supercat.

Ace

Aceroo

Batman

Billy Batson   [Captain Marvel's true identity]

Captain Marvel

Champ

Chen   [Chinese for "great"]

Clark   [Kent]

Conan   [The Barbarian]

Daredevil

Dr. Strange

The Flash   [Comic-strip recreation of the winged Mercury]

Flash Gordon

Flummox

Green Lantern

Hawkman   [Winged phantom]

Hotshot

Hulk

Ibis   ["The Invincible"]

James Bond

Jungle Jim

King Kull

Lois Lane

Lone Ranger

Magnífico   [Spanish for "swell," "excellent"]

Maximilian   [Latin for "greatest"; var.: Max, Maxie, Maximo, Maxy, Mack]

Moxie

007

Popeye

Prince Namor   [Atlantis-born hero in the comic strip The Submariner]

Prince Valiant

Robin   [Batman's sidekick]

Shazam   [The word that adds two feet and ten years to Billy Batson in Captain Marvel comic strip]

Sheena   [Queen of the Jungle]

Silver Surfer

Spectre   [Green-caped comic-strip character]

Thor

The Torch

Triton

The Web

The White Streak

Whizcat

Zorro

The Space Cadet

Like its close relative the Supercat, this cat feels a certain kinship with creatures of the outer world. It is convinced that its grandfather came from the planet Krypton. Such cosmic ancestry explains (to those who want to know) why it possesses the highest form of intelligence.

Occasionally, the Space Cadet will make an attempt to return to its place of origin. It will search out a launching pad for that purpose and try blasting off skyward like a rocket. If it doesn't succeed, the Space Cadet will try again. And again. There are some who wish it would succeed . . .

Admiral Motti   [Charge of the Death Star defense system in Star Wars]

Andy   [Space ship robot in the TV series Quark]

Arrakis   [Planet setting in Dune]

Asteroid

Astro

Barbarella   [Jane Fonda science-fiction movie]

Caprica   [Planet destroyed in TV series Battlestar Galactica]

Centurion   [Spaceship]

Chani   [Robot in the movie Devil Girl from Mars]

Clavius   [Space station in the movie 2001: A Space Odyssey]

Cold Eye   [Of Moon Cresta]

Cresta   [Of Moon Cresta]

Davama   [Home planet in the movie Not of This Earth]

Droid

Electro [Robot in Marvel Mystery Comics]

Elektro [Robot created by Westinghouse]

E.T.

Fireball

Galactica

Galaxian

Garwor [Warrior in Wor]

General Willord [Commandant of the rebel forces in Star Wars]

Gorf [Space invader]

Gorfian

Gremlin

Han Solo [Of Star Wars]

Jedi

Lando Kalresian [Of Star Wars]

Laser

Luna [Spaceship in the movie Destination Moon]

Martian

Meteor

Nostromo [Interstellar ship in the movie Alien]

Ork [Mork's home planet in the TV series]

Phobo [Martian in Phobos]

Phoenix [Space invader]

Princess Leia [Heroine of Star Wars]

Pushky [Opponent of clouds and other pushkies in Pushky]

Retro

Samuel   [Protagonist in Air Raid]

Sark   [The red warrior in Tron]

Scorpion   [Of Centipede]

See-Threepio   [Droid in Star Wars]

Sega   [Of Centipede]

Skywalker   [Hero of Star Wars]

Spectar   [Smuggler in videogame Targ]

Spider   [Of Centipede]

Spock

Super-Fly   [Of Moon Cresta]

Targ   [Videogame]

Tatooine   [Planet in Star Wars]

Thorwor   [Warrior in Wor]

Tron   [Protagonist of Tron]

Vulcan   [Mr. Spock's home planet in Star Trek]

Warbird   [Of Phoenix]

Warlord   [Videogame]

Warp

Wor   [Of Wizard of Oz]

Worling   [Denizen of the dungeon in Wor]

Worluk   [Denizen in Wor]

Worrier   [Denizen of the dungeon in Wor]

Wummel   [Ramship in videogame Targ]

Yonda   [Spaceship in the TV series The Fantastic Journey]

Yori   [Flynn's friend in Tron]

The Boss

This cat expects you to be at its beck and call at all times and to do as it meows. It rules the household with an iron paw. If it wants you to move over on the livingroom couch, it will tell you so in no uncertain terms: if a gentle nudge won't do, a few well-aimed slaps will. If you take up too much of the bed, it will walk over your face until you wake up. Clearly, the word "no" is missing from this cat's vocabulary.

Adalia [Old German for "noble one"]

Adele [Old German for "noble"; var.: Adeline, Adela, Aline]

Admiral

Aldrich [From the Teutonic "wise ruler"; var.: Eldridge]

Alexander [The Great]

Ali [Arabic for "Jehovah"]

Ali Baba [From Arabian Nights]

Allah

Almira [Arabic for "exalted"]

Alpha [Greek for "first one"; var.: Alfa]

Amun [Egyptian god]

Artemis [Center of feline worship in Ancient Egypt]

Aughra [Watcher of Heaven in The Dark Crystal]

August [Latin for "majestic one"; fem.: Augusta]

Augustus [Latin for "exalted"]

Avatar [Manifestation of Divine Being]

Baron, Baroness

Basil [From the Latin "kingly"; var.: Basilio, Basilius]

Bast [Egyptian god]

Beniolji [Indian chief]

Brunhild [Wife of Gunther in <u>Nibelungenlied</u>]

Bubastis [Greek name for Bast]

Caligula [Roman emperor]

Capitaine [French for "captain"]

Capitano [Italian for "captain"]

Caporal [Spanish for "corporal"]

Captain

Cedric [From the Old English "chieftain"]

CEO

Chandea [Priestess of Delphi]

Chato [Indian chief]

Chauncey [From the Middle English "chancellor"]

Chen [Chinese for "great"]

Chevalier [French knight or nobleman]

Chief

Churchill

Colonel

Conrad [From the Old German "bold"]

Count, Countess

Cyrus [Persian for "throne"]

Czar, Czarina

Dagda [Celtic god able to separate himself into twelve distinct and powerful entities]

Dirigo [Latin for "I guide, I direct"; motto of Maine]

Don, Doña [Spanish title of respect]

218

Donald [Gaelic for "ruler of the world"; var.: Donaldo]

Duchess, Duke

Egbert [First king of England]

Elmer [From the Old English "noble and famous"]

Emperor

Enrique [From the Teutonic "ruler of the home"]

General

Geronimo [Indian chief]

Genghis Khan [Mongolian conqueror]

Greybeard [Indian chief]

Gunther [King of Burgundy in Nibelungenlied]

Hannibal [Carthaginian general]

Hera [Latin for "ruling lady"]

Hoypt [Yiddish for "chief"]

Impresario

Isis [Egyptian goddess]

Jeremy [From the Hebrew "appointed of Jehovah"]

Jeromel [From the Latin "holy name"]

Kim [From the Old English "chief," "ruler"]

King Arthur

Kirk [James T. Kirk of Star Trek]

Kubla Khan [Founder of the Mongolian dynasty]

Lama

LeRoy [French for "king"]

Li Shoe   [Chinese for "deity"]

Logan   [Indian chief]

Maharajah, Maharani

Mahask   [Indian chief]

Majesty

Major

Marquis

Marshall

Maxwell   [From the Old English "influential"]

Melvin   [From the Celtic "chief"; var.: Melvyn]

Michael   [Hebrew for "who is like God"; var.: Mickey, Mike, Michele, Mitchell]

Midas

Mohammed   [Arabic for "praised"]

Mullah   [Turkish judge]

Napoleon

Omar   [Turkish for "most high"]

Oncpapa   [Indian chief]

Patrick   [From the Latin "noble one"; var.: Paddy, Patrizio]

Pocahontas   [Indian princess]

Premier

Primo   [Italian for "chief"]

Red Cloud   [Indian chief]

Reginald   [From the Old English "mighty and powerful"; var.: Rinaldo, Reinaldo]

Rex [Latin for "king"]

Ricarda [From the Old English "powerful ruler"]

Richard [From the Old German "powerful ruler"; var.: Ricky, Ricardo]

Ronald, Ronalda ["Mighty power"]

Roy [From the French roi, "king"]

Sacajawea [Indian scout for Lewis and Clark]

Sachem [Indian chief]

Sakima [Indian word for "king"]

Sebastian [From Latin "the august one"]

Shag-ti [Chinese god of heaven; head of celestial bureaucracy]

Shaman [Priest and magician]

Shiek

Shogun

Spotted Tail [Indian chief]

Squire

Sultan

Swami

Ukko [Supreme god in Finnish myth]

Valdemar [From the Old German "famous ruler"]

Waldemar [Scandinavian for "famous ruler"]

Walter [From the Old German "army ruler"]

Xerxes [From the Persian "royal prince"]

The Dancer

Cats like to trip the light fantastic whether there's music or not.
But they differ in their approaches to the art. The more traditional
types pretty much stick with the classic two-step. The more

adventurous will try their paws at more elaborate moves—the turkey trot, the Charleston, the hootchy-kootchy, or the soft-shoe, for example. Some may even try ballet, kicking their paws smartly together as they pirouette into the air. And why not? Anything people can do, cats can do better. After all, they have twice as many legs.

Alima [Arabic for "expert dancer"]

Allemande [German dance]

Apache [French dance]

Arabesque [Ballet position]

Astaire

Balanchine

Ballo [Fifteenth-century Italian dancing master]

Baryshnikov

Batterie [Beating steps]

Bayadere [Dancing girl in India]

Bolero [Spanish dance]

Boogaloo [Hip-swiveling dance]

Cabriole [A ballet leap in which one leg beats against the other]

Can-Can

Cantico [Ceremonial Indian dance]

Capriole [Upward leap made by a trained horse]

Caracole [Sudden half-turn made by a horse]

Cha-Cha

Charleston

Conchina [Japanese dance]

Conga [Cuban dance]

Contra [American country dance]

Cotillion [A square dance, French for "petticoat"]

Fandango [Spanish dance; the word means "go and dance"]

Flamenco [Andalusian folk dance]

Fling [Lively Scottish dance]

Fox trot

Fred [Astaire]

Frug

Furlana [Italian dance]

Gallopade [Brisk dance]

Gambado [Dance step, meaning "flourish"]

Gopak [Russian dance]

Hula [Hawaiian dance]

Hustle

Jeté [Turn]

Jig [Solo Irish dance]

Jitterbug

Jota [Spanish dance]

Juba [Afro-American folk dance]

Lindy

Lundu [African folk dance]

Makarova

Mambo [Cuban dance]

Mazurka [Polish dance]

224

Merengue [Dominican dance]

Minuet

Nijinski

Nureyev

Pachanga [Caribbean dance]

Pavlova

Pirouette

Piva [Italian folk dance]

Pointe [Pointed toe in ballet]

Polka [Bohemian dance]

Promenade

Ragtime

Rumba

Samba [Brazilian dance]

Shimmy [Jazz dance]

Tango

Tarantella [Neapolitan dance]

Twist

Vedda [A convulsive dance to achieve a state of ecstasy]

Waltz

Watusi

FIGURE SKATING

Lobe [Semicircle]   Mazurka [Jump]   Wilson [Jump]

Loop [Movement]   Spiral [Freestyle body position]

The Great Lover

This macho cat takes pride in his irresistibility to the opposite sex—a view not always shared by both parties. The Great Lover is not about to enter into a philosophical discussion on the subject, however. It's action he is looking for.

Should the encounter lead to a litter of cute little kittens (as is often the case), the Great Lover makes it his business to move on. It's not that he is against the propagation of his own species. As a matter of fact, it pleases him to see his own image multiplied. However, the decent fellow that he is, he feels that concentration on just one female would be grossly unfair to all the others.

Ace

Adam

Adonis

Amoroso

Antony   [Cleopatra's lover]

Apollo

Beau Brummel

Bluebeard

Buckeroo

Caballero   [Spanish for "knight"]

Casanova

Cuckoo   [Bird associated with inconstancy and faithlessness]

Cupid

Cyrano de Bergerac

Daddy

Dandy

Dazzler

Desperado

Ding Dong

Don Juan

Ego

Erato

Gable

Gigolo

Hanky-Panky

Hef [Hugh Hefner]

Henry VIII

Honcho

Hustler

Jockey

Libido

Lothario

Magnifico

Matador

Mellors [Gardener in Lady Chatterley's Lover]

Othello

Ovid [Roman author of books on love]

Papa

Playboy

Punch

Rake

Romeo

Seraglio [Palace of Sultan and his harem]

Sheik

Tom Jones [Sower of wild oats in novel by Henry Fielding]

Valentine [Var.: Valentin, Valentino]

Whiskers

Willie

The Computer Wizard

High-tech fascinates cats, especially those of the new generation.
Space mice on the screen make them sit up and watch. And the
bleeps emanating from the machine keep them awake for several
minutes at a time.

Word processors are particularly appealing: cases have been reported of entire paragraphs thrown on the screen by cats expertly working the console. Unfortunately their writing is rarely good enough for publication. That's because cats are notoriously poor spellers.

Ada [High-level programming language]

Adis [Automatic Data Interchange System]

Adres [Army Data Retrieval System]

Agris [Agricultural Information System]

Aglinet [Agricultural Libraries Information Network]

Agricola [Database by the U.S. Department of Agriculture]

Algol [Algorithmic Oriented Language]

Alu [Arithmetic and logic unit]

Amacus [Automated Microfilm Aperture Card Update System]

Analog [Representation of information]

Ansi [American National Standards Institute]

Antiope [French videotex]

Apilit [Database]

Arpanet [Resource-sharing computer network]

Artemis [Automatic Retrieval of Text]

Aru [Audio response unit]

Asca [Automatic Subject Citation Alert]

Bead [Small program for specific function]

Bim [Beginning of information marker]

Binary [System using two alternatives]

Bit [Binary digit]

Blip [Unwanted signal on the screen]

Byte [Group of bits]

Cam [Computer Aided Manufacturing Systems]

Camis [Computer Assisted Make-up System]

Chip [Thin slice of silicon]

Cobol [Common Business Oriented Language]

Codee [Coder-decoder]

Coden [Five-character code]

Compertino [A computer-oriented town near San Francisco]

Comstar [Communications satellite provided by Comsat]

Costar [On-line information system]

Cursor [A light indicator on a VDU]

Cycle [Sequence of operations]

DC [Digital Computer—also Direct Current]

DD [Digital Data or Data Demand]

Digicom [Digital communication system]

Dip [Form of chip]

Diskette

Docfax [Facsimile transmission]

Dolby [Noise reduction system]

Dor [Digital Optical Recording]

Emerac [Computer in TV series Voyage to the Bottom of the Sea]

Eprom [Erasable memory]

Esi [Externally specified index]

Fortran [High-level computer language]

Gigo [Garbage in, garbage out]

Laser

Lexis [Lexicography Information System]

Lilo [Last in, last out]

Megabyte [A million bytes]

Micro

Microchip

Micron [One millionth of a meter]

Orion [On-line retrieval of information over a network]

Patolis [Patent On-line Information System]

Quicktran [Quick for Fortran]

Ram [Random Access Memory]

Ramis [Random Access Management Information System]

Rax [Remote access]

Recol [Retrieval Command Language]

Remstar [Electronic Microfilm Storage Transmission and Retrieval]

Rom [Read Only Memory]

Salinet [Satellite Library Information Network]

Sector [Smallest unit of memory]

Semcor [Semantic Correlation]

Silicon

Som [Start of Message]

Spooler [Software controlling usage]

Vogad [Voice Operated Gain Adjustment Device]

Where Were You Born, Cat?

Your beloved cat's birthplace may yet be a well-kept secret. If that is the case you can only make an educated guess about the cat's origin. Go ahead and try—and use the information for inspiration. Your cat will be happy to learn that somewhere in this world a city or a state has adopted its name. For as far as the cat is concerned, it is never the other way around.

STATES

Amboy [New Jersey]

Apache [Arizona]

Bayou [Mississippi]

Bluebonnet [Texas]

Bowie [Arkansas]

Buckeye [Ohio]

Buzzard [Georgia]

Cajun [Louisiana]

Cal [California]

Chinook [Washington]

Columbine [Colorado]

Cooper [Wisconsin]

Creole [Louisiana]

Dakota [North Dakota]

Delly [Delaware]

Dirigo [Maine]

El Dorado [California]

Empire [New York]

En Dee [North Dakota]

Excelsior [New York]

Gator [Florida]

Ginny [Virginia]

Goober [Georgia]

Greeny [Vermont]

Gun Flint [Rhode Island]

Hampshire [New Hampshire]

Hawkeye [Iowa]

Hoosier [Indiana]

Ida [Idaho]

Illinoy [Illinois]

Ioway [Iowa]

Joisey [New Jersey]

Kentuck [Kentucky]

Knickerbocker [New York]

Little Mary [Maryland]

Massa [Massachusetts]

Massy [Massachusetts]

Mich [Michigan]

234

Minnie [Minnesota]

Mizzou [Missouri]

Monty [Montana]

Nebrasky [Nebraska]

New Mex [New Mexico]

N.J. [New Jersey]

Nutmeg [Connecticut]

Ocotillo [Arizona]

Okie [Oklahoma]

Orange [Florida]

Palmetto [South Carolina]

Penn [Pennsylvania]

Pennsy [Pennsylvania]

Rhody [Rhode Island]

Sagebrush [Wyoming]

Sagehen [Nevada]

S.C. [South Carolina]

S.D. [South Dakota]

Sego Lily [Utah]

Sunflower [Kansas]

Tenny [Tennessee]

Tex [Texas]

Tucko [North Carolina]

Tucky [Kentucky]

Virginny [Virginia]

Wash [Washington]

Webfoot [Oregon]

CITIES

Angeleno [Los Angeles]

Aqua [Abilene, Texas]

Athens [Boston]

Balto, Balty [Baltimore]

Big D [Dallas]

Bow Wow [Boston]

Casey [Kansas City]

Chi [Chicago]

Cincy [Cincinnati]

Cisco [San Francisco]

D.C. [Washington, D.C.]

Frisco [San Francisco]

Gotham [New York]

Hogopolis [Chicago]

K.C. [Kansas City]

L.A. [Los Angeles]

Looey [St. Louis]

Loop, Looper [Chicago]

Los [Los Angeles]

Manhattador [Manhattan]

N.O. [New Orleans]

Nobby [Nob Hill]

Ollie [Hollywood]

Palmetto [Charleston]

Phil, Philly [Philadelphia]

Pigopolis [Chicago]

Pitt [Pittsburgh]

Porkopolis [Burlington]

Rocky [Rochester]

Sisco [San Francisco]

Walla [Walla Walla]

The Obedient Cat

There is no such animal.